Adventures in Subbing: The Life and Times of a Classroom Mercenary

M. C. Shaw

Preface

"*My father thinks you're an amazing wordsmith. My mother, on the other hand, thinks your tattoos are trashy.*"

- Andy P., 12th grade, Class of 2016

"*Mr. Shaw is simply unprofessional: he is rude to other teachers and does not take feedback well. I would prefer not to see him on our campus anymore. Students love him, and I don't know why.*"

- Margaret Gedenson, Principal's Secretary/Last Living Dinosaur

Dedication

This book is dedicated to the incredible teachers in my life, whether they were teachers in title or not:

My mother, who taught me to go again until it's right, take no shit and *"don't bury hatchets...bury bodies."*

My father, who taught me the importance of building solid relationships, and that *"it doesn't cost anything to be nice."*

My godmother Marcia, who unquestionably nurtured my love of reading and comedy, and when in doubt, always told me to ask myself *"what the hell did you do that for!?"*

My fairy godparents Jennifer and Mark, who helped transform a goofy, awkward teen into a goofy, awkward man, and who taught me to *"always set an example...and never drink out of the loaner cup."*

My wife, who was not only instrumental in pushing me to be my best possible self, but also my biggest cheerleader during my teaching exams. She is obviously my favorite person, whether we're going on spooky ghost adventures or just binge-watching shows.

It's also dedicated to Jesse Salbato, one of the loudest voices continually pushing me to commit this to writing. And to the rest of you who clamored for it: I definitely wouldn't have done this without your support (or fantastic art)!

This book is specifically dedicated to teachers who have modeled incredible strategies over the past ten years. And if you're *not* a teacher, please do something nice for a teacher in your life–they deserve it. And for the love of all things holy, don't just give them a $10 Starbucks card in a generic "thank you" card. A handwritten letter of heartfelt appreciation fuels us better than a half-caff double soy latte with light foam and a caramel drizzle. Cash is good, too.

Last, but not least, this is dedicated to Kevin Smith, who inspired me to "just do the damn thing" all those years ago.

And thank **you**, dear reader. This whole thing has been in the works for more than eleven years now. Thank you for taking a chance on this rambling account of jackassery.

Introduction

So You Wanna Be a Substitute?

A substitute's job is thankless, truly.

As I hear it, back in the day, all you needed to be a sub was a relatively clean record and the ability to spell and add passably. Because of this, there are a shitload of retiree-aged substitutes in the system who eke out a living in the most passive way possible. There are subs I knew personally, who would regularly fall asleep in class; others that would spend the day reading the newspaper and not even remotely engaging the kids. That's *their* hustle, I guess.

Any substitute teachers born after 1975, however, needed to pass a set of state tests ($220ish if you pass 'em the first time), a background test, and a Livescan set of fingerprints (approximately $110), *and* pay another $120 annually to keep your credential updated. So that means approximately once a year, you'll work an assignment for FREE in order to keep your credential active. Neat.

If you're lucky, you'll pull down between $80-115 per day for an assignment (pre-tax), with the potential of adding or subtracting $30 for including/removing an extra period in your day; and unless you pay for hack software like SubFinder, finding work can be incredibly inconsistent.

And yet, even with all the prerequisites for employment, there's absolutely zero formal training (aside from a couple of mandatory "hey buddy, don't be a rapist" online videos). You're expected to come into the assignment with a sunny disposition and a *"can DO!"* attitude.

When you arrive at the school, the only people who want to talk to you are the admins; the teachers all treat you like you're transient and expendable...but that's because you are.

You're essentially replaceable; thus, *you need to make yourself essential*--and that's the sub hustle in a nutshell. I've known subs to correct homework and exams, scrub down desks, wipe off whiteboards, vacuum the room, and leave notes stapled to Starbucks gift cards, with their phone number written down "for next time." Substitutes will bad-mouth each other to the teachers and staff in hopes that it'll give them a leg up on the competition, and they rarely look out for each other. There's no camaraderie in the sub-pool because, for every assignment that *you* get, someone else *doesn't* get one.

Most potential substitute teachers imagine subbing like doing a single-day gig in a third-grade, neurotypical classroom: do some painting, maybe read a Ramona book, take an hour nap at lunch, teach some times tables, color a couple of handouts, and usher the kiddos out the door at 2:45. Beautiful, right?

The reality is, subs are shunted into whatever classroom needs coverage, and you rarely get to pick where you go. The phone system is skewed to contact "preferred" teachers first and move down the line according to who is geographically closest to the site. Sure, you can decline the sub assignment they're calling you about...but I rarely got a same-day callback with a different assignment option. Simply put: if you're offered a job, you should take that job. New substitutes who have yet to ingratiate themselves with the school's secretary (someone you should

ABSOLUTELY make friends with), often end up at the bottom of the list, which tends to be the...well...let's call them *less preferred* classrooms.

If you're a new sub, there are all sorts of apps you can purchase for a monthly/annual fee that will notify you when a position opens, allowing you to queue yourself up before the other substitute teachers. It's absolutely worth the $15 monthly fee if you plan on doing this for an extended amount of time, and was the reason I was able to make a living for the first couple months. Of course, in a perfect world, you shouldn't *have* to pay for an app that hacks the system, but here we are. *"H@CK TH3 PL@N3T!"* it is!

But I digress.

These "less than optimal" classroom assignments are not unlike the Thunderdome: students often have "moderate to severe" level of disability ("MOD/SEV"), are severely emotionally disturbed ("SED"), not to mention all of the other various and sundry "special day" classes that are often imposed upon new substitutes. Not surprisingly, many end up leaving the profession due to these early assignments.

I remember stories of petite women (not that gender matters, but it's a fact) in their early 20s, who called the school resource officers (AKA SROs, school cops–or NARCs if you ask the kids) and shut themselves in a closet while the kids reenacted Maurice Sendak's Wild Rumpus in the classroom, throwing papers into the air and class materials on the ground until someone eventually came in to stop them.

THIS was the world I was born into; my first "official" long-term substitute classroom was a (supposedly) maximum-security gig with two "security support" assistants in the classroom with me. Again, there was ZERO training from the district, and zero explanation of what I was getting myself into–aside from a list of unexplained acronyms attached to the assignment.

What SHOULD be taught to all potential substitutes in this environment is de-escalation, empathy, and basic communication skills. Instead, it was a "learn by doing" model that shattered the resolve of some people...and tempered others. Or, as my dear friend Mike is fond of saying "adversity can be the stone that crushes, or it can be the stone that sharpens." And let me tell you: a *lot* of shiny, new substitute teachers were crushed.

At the end of each day, there's no real support. No extra counseling. No debrief. Just a heaping helping of "leave your keys at the main desk and sign the clipboard on your way out."

Every single day was a battle, and if you walked away unscathed, by God, you should consider it a victory.

This is a true account of chaos, coupled with the directions I wish I had before starting. There's learning to be had–and a LOT I wish I could tell myself, with Marty McFly-like introspection. But then again, had I not suffered through those blunders, I wouldn't be the teacher I am today. As you read this chronicle, there are going to be some chuckles, some wry smiles...maybe even some tears. But there's also going to be a *whole* lot of cringe.

My hope is that this account will serve as a kind of "don't do this" with a dash of "this worked well" and a palate cleanser of "and here's what I SHOULD have done."

So come along with me as I grimace at my past deeds (and many misdeeds) throughout my first few years of substitute teaching. These are all daily entries I jotted down each day, as well as some as teacher notes, and some just because I didn't want to forget them.[1] As a result, these accounts tend to be a "warts and all" approach to the day's events. They'll also serve as somewhat of an evolution of mind, from a brand new sub who was thrown into a wild situation and transformed into a battle-tested teacher who loves his job and his students.

I hope that, by taking this trip again, we can learn from the past together, in order to strengthen our future.

Welcome to the Thunderdome.

Welcome to the sub life.

February 12th, 2013:

"The Future of Target and Radio Shack in Sub Saharan Africa" (*per Jenny*)

I just sat through 90 minutes of AP World Studies presentations on international socioeconomics.

These are high school seniors, mind you.

I had to reproduce this one word for word, which wasn't hard, because she was reading off her Google Slides notes verbatim.

"In general, in case you didn't know, Africa is pretty poor…especially, like, Middle Africa. More poor people means little to less cellphones. Less cellphones means no demand. No demand means there probably won't be an Apple store in their mall anytime soon. There will probably be a Target or Radio Shack though."

At the end of class, she came over and asked in pure, abject seriousness, "awesome, right?!"

We're ALL doomed.

Chapter 1:

"Uphill Both Ways"

Prior to my stint as a substitute teacher in March of 2012, I spent ten years as a copy editor at a fair-to-middling publishing company. As a child, I just *barely* tested positive under the threshold of attention deficit disorder and mild dyslexia, and I would often read quicker and more comprehensively by turning the book upside down. Even with partial deafness, mild processing issues, and attention challenges, I developed a massive love of reading. And though my disabilities followed me into my adult life, here I was: editor extraordinaire and making $55+K per year to read and write long-form articles. I was moving up in the world!

At least...until I was unceremoniously laid off.

For the first time since I was 15, I found myself unemployed for over a month. As I struggled to figure out my next step, Scout, the teacher that my then-wife Tammy worked alongside, suggested that I come in and do a guest lecture for her kiddos.

I mean, I was meeting Tammy for lunch a couple times a week anyway, so why not extend the visit a little longer and talk to the kiddos? Plus, it was an English class for students with "mild-to-moderate" disabilities, which was *exactly* the banner I sailed under during my high school years!

I had an absolute blast hanging out with her kids; they were fun, asked great questions, and genuinely seemed shocked that someone with a reading/attention disability could get a job reading all day...and be paid good money for doing it!

One guest lecture turned into four, and Scout would tell me how the kids would ask daily "when would Mr. S be coming back again?" Being in the classroom, and talking about editing jobs and writing work, helped normalize that an adult with several disabilities can, in fact, end up with a good-paying career.

At the end of the fourth session, "wanna do another guest lecture" turned into "WAIT! You should take over my classroom when I go on maternity leave!"

I gulped comically. "Wait...*what*?"

The way she mentioned it so casually made me think that applying to be a substitute was as easy as applying to be a barista, and given that I had held several writing jobs in the 20 years, I figured it would be a breeze.

Sure, I'd need to do a background check to prove that I don't have a history of suddenly attacking children or adults, as well as provide three or four letters of recommendation from other business professionals saying that I'm not a trash goblin that bites when cornered. Plus, a copy of all my inoculation records, so in the event of said bite, they knew I was up-to-date on all my shots.

At least, that's how Scout packaged it to me. "I'll call Tracy in the morning and have her send you the paperwork."

Easy peasy, lemon squeezy, right?

It ended up being a logistical nightmare.

In order to become a substitute teacher, you needed to show proof of passing the Grammar/Spelling/Punctuation (GSP) test, as well as a basic skills assessment for high school math, essay writing, and reading. Then, I needed to apply for a substitute teaching credential through the state, get LiveScan fingerprinted, and pay for certification, all of which I had to pay out of pocket.

The biggest challenge in all this was time: I had less than a month to get it all together...and yet somehow, I did. I crash-studied, took practice tests, wrote out flashcards, and actually hired a tutor to help me with the math I couldn't wrap my brain around. It was an absolute whirlwind that had me literally praying every night that I was doing the right thing.

And somehow, against all odds, I pulled it off with two days to spare.

Unfortunately, what Scout neglected to tell me was that the final boss in this terrible HR video game was the district itself. Up until this point, I had thought that teachers ultimately chose what substitute they used. That was *definitely* not the case.

Two weeks after turning all of my exhaustive paperwork in, I called Tracy in the district's HR office to check on the status of my application.

"Hello?" Tracy's voice was that of someone who drinks coffee in the morning and cheap scotch at night, with that smug ex-smoker rasp that was just *begging* someone to test her. I could tell from her tone that she was done with the conversation before it had even started.

Time to pour on the charm. Deep breath. "Good morning, Tracy. This is MacArthur Shaw. Scout's friend? I was calling to check on my paperwork."

"You need HR."

"Aren't *you* HR?"

"You need a *different* HR person."

"Yes, but before I check in with them..."

"YOU. NEED. TO. SPEAK. TO. SOMEONE. ELSE." I imagined her angrily jabbing a pen into a yellow steno pad to punctuate each word. *Click.* I was transferred without warning.

"Good morning, human resources, this is Kelly!" This chipper voice was the polar opposite of Tracy. I hastily explained myself, and asked Kelly about my status. "Oh, was this a special circumstance? We don't usually hire new subs until August, and our offers to return (the promissory letter that substitutes fill out, saying that they plan on returning) already went out for this year. But yes, I see we received your paperwork. It's up to Tracy whether she wants to activate you."

"Oh. Hmmm. Ok. Maybe I could..."

"I'll transfer you! One moment!"

"NO! WAIT..."

"HELLLLLLO?" Tracy growled into the handset. Great.

"Hi Tracy! It's Mac Sh..."

"WHAT ELSE DO YOU NEED?"

"Well, I was just informed that HR received my paperwork, but they need you to green-light it before it can be processed..."

I could hear her taut, joyless grin through the phone. "AND *WHY* WOULD I DO THAT?"

"Well, I understand that Scout personally requested me to cover for her materni..."

"TRUST ME, WE HAVE PLENTY OF VIABLE SUBSTITUTES. BUT I'VE NEVER HAD A TEACHER REQUEST SOMEONE SO ADAMANTLY BEFORE. WHAT MAKES YOU SO SPECIAL?"

"Well, I guess you'll just have to come watch me teach to find out."

Silence. I could hear a nasal exhale that may have been a laugh... Or was it exasperation?

"FINE. YOU GET A CONDITIONAL ACCEPTANCE *FOR THIS JOB ONLY.* AFTER THAT, WE'LL REEVALUATE." Which honestly, sounded like she was going to can me the day Scout's assignment ended. But I was IN!

"Thank you." I probably should have said something more clever, but I didn't want to poke that bear any more than I already had.

My first day taking over Scout's class was a dream; the kids all knew me, and since I had taught them before, it was like slipping into a comfortable pair of shoes. The class designation was mild/moderate disability, so most of the students were pretty self-directed.

Every day, I'd somehow get all the kids to participate...all except Carlo.

Carlo was never rude, but he'd just nod at me and smile when I'd talk to him. He would never interact independently--with other students or with me. During read-alouds, he'd just shake his head when it was his turn to read, then look expectantly at the kid next to him until they took over.

I noticed that his mother would always pick him up late, and I often saw her pulling up as I walked to my car. After the fourth day, I flagged her down as I was leaving.

"Hi! Are you Carlo's mom?" She nodded and smiled, just like he did. She spoke haltingly. *"Only a little English, ok?"* She held up her fingers, pinching them close together. Her voice had a sweet lilt to it.

"Sure!" I mirrored her big smile. "I'm wondering about Carlo. In class? He doesn't want to..."

She waved her hand dismissively. *"Just have him work packets."*

I must have furrowed my eyebrows, because she said *"Oh no. I not mad! It's ok. Him just like, retarded, ok? Like...you understand?"*

Carlo was nodding and smiling next to her, but when she hit the R-word, I saw his demeanor shift. He *completely* understood what she was saying. And we both cringed noticeably.

Before I could interject, she trilled *"Ok! I'm go now. Thank you for help!"* And with that, she drove away, leaving me confused and more than a little frustrated.

The next day while doing morning check-in, I decided to take great pains to include Carlo in our class discussion. Same smile and head shake. No other communication. Damn it.

Many of the kids would eat in the classroom during lunch since it was a safe, "chill" space. Most of them would mess around on their phones, read comic books, or just chat in groups. It was a pretty accepting space for all types of conversations.

Midway through devouring my sandwich, my phone rings, and it's the Kia dealership. My Soul had crapped out earlier in the week, and I was hoping it was a warranty issue. The mechanic said they still needed to run more tests. It wasn't stellar news.

As I hung up, I noticed Carlo staring at me raptly.

I waved to him. "What's up, buddy?" He continued to stare at my face, searching for meaning. "Oh, that was just the dealership. I had a problem with my car..."

Carlo grinned "Soul's not a good car."

This was literally the first time I had heard him speak a complete sentence. I stared at him, flabbergasted.

"What?"

"You said to the guy. Kia Soul. Sealed engine. Hard to fix. All plastic. Not good." His staccato delivery was all business.

My heart was racing. *Alright, be cool. Don't get too excited, or else you're gonna scare him off!*

"Well...ok. What kind of car should I get?"

"Classic car. Ford maybe? Old. Good. Steel. Stock body. They make sense. Easier to fix."

I nodded. "What do you know about fixing cars?"

His eyes lit up. "I work with my uncle. Rotate tires and do rotors, bleed brakes, and switch engines. Everything." He grinned.

Unreal. I spent the last week trying to figure out whether the kid was verbal or not, only to find out that he could *totally* speak...he just didn't see a reason to.

For the remainder of the semester, I worked closely with Carlo, and when we looked into summer volunteer jobs, he told me that when he grew up, he wanted to be a mechanic. But not just *any* mechanic, "an *ASE certified* mechanic who worked on imports, because that's where the *big* money is!"

When the students presented their final work, I had Carlo talk about the steps involved with getting an ASE certification and which places in the city were the best options. To better help his mom understand, I made sure he was using lots of visuals and encouraged him to translate whenever he thought it would be helpful. His mother watched, but it was clear that this was boring her to tears.

Carlo had, far and away, the most detailed presentation, with video clips, pictures of him and his uncle working on cars, and even websites that offered more information on getting ASE certified. When he concluded, the applause in the room was deafening, and he beamed from the front of the class.

As other parents and students filed out, I made sure to point out Carlo's success to his mom. She shook her head and said *"But it's just cars. It was good. It was fine."* Her tone was dismissive, and I'm glad he wasn't around to hear her.

I think about Carlo whenever I have a challenging parent interaction now. Back then, I didn't think to have an interpreter sit down with her, to help her understand the right terms to use with her kid...but also to encourage him to pursue a career working with cars, since that's where his passion is.

Again, this was my first experience subbing, and it was incredible. The environment was thoughtful, relatively nurturing, and positive. It wasn't until I left that particular charter school that I discovered how green I truly was.

Chapter 2:

"Exampling The Limited Possible"

After I finished out the year covering Scout's maternity leave, I was plugged into the main subbing pool, not only for Scout's charter school but also for all of the schools in the district.

My account of the next three years has a caveat: unlike Scout's class, where I pretty much had free reign to work with the kids and co-develop their lessons, the district assignments were a *lot* different. Though there were some exceptions, our job was pretty much to observe the classroom events, pass out work, take attendance, make sure that all students were accounted for during the day... and make sure nobody died.

Much of my first few years subbing was spent observing and taking notes, since a substitute's job is to manage the class in the teacher's absence--*not* to be a replacement teacher.

I say this because the first couple of chapters, to quote Ryan Sickler, "highlight the lowlights," *especially* since I had zero idea what to expect. We were explicitly told *not* to intervene in the event of a problem and were instructed to call for support, and document, document, *document* every occurrence we witnessed.

6:40 a.m. the following Monday, I got my first automated sub call to cover for an art class at Tate, a nearby public high school. It should be cake, right? I mean, if you're going to ease into the world of substitute teaching for people that *aren't* your good friends, art class seems like a pretty great place to do it.

I had never been on this campus before, so I was acutely aware that a 6'1, nearly 300lb gorilla in an ill-fitting button-down shirt and khakis will be scrutinized the moment they walk onto campus. I somehow made it past the school guard...probably due to the massive thermos and lunch bag I was clutching to my chest.

The secretary, a prim-looking older woman, handed me the classroom keys and the attendance folder and stuck a Post-It on the cover, with 91132 written on it in bright red Sharpie.

"You won't be subbing *only* art today--you'll actually be subbing for three social studies classes and one art class. If you need anything," she chirped in her singsongy voice, "just call that extension there and we'll help you! Have a great day!"

I left the office a little confused but, ultimately, hopeful. Social studies could be fun, right? When I got to the classroom, the instructions were to "put the DVD in the player behind the desk and play the first hour of 'The Blind Side' for each class." The only problem was, there was no DVD to be found. Not in the player, not on the desk, not anywhere. And the kids were starting to filter through the door. Great.

The secretary's sing-songy voice echoed in my head *"just call that extension and we'll help you!"* So I picked up the handset and punched in 91132. Imagine my surprise when the phone rang twice, followed by a stoic voice asking "911, what's your emergency?"

My insides turned to ice. "AHH! Sorry, I'm uh, I dialed the wrong number. Accidentally."

The dispatcher exhaled loudly. "You *accidentally* dialed 911?"

"Believe it or not, yes." I could hear her eyes rolling through the phone. "Fine. Try not to do it again. Have a nice day."

Shaking and red-faced, I put the handset back on the cradle while all the kids stared at me.

Cool.

Cool, cool, cool, cooooool.

"Okay! Good morning, everyone! My name is, uh, Mr. Shaw and I'll be covering for your teacher," I glanced down at the name on the file: Chris Palmer. "Covering for Mr..."

"*MISS!*" a girl in the front row hissed. The class giggled.

"Right. Uh. *Miss* Palmer. Okay. Let's take attendance?"

When I was halfway through the list of 30-plus students, the classroom door crashed open, and a portly school resource officer ran in, glancing around wildly.

"*WHO* DIALED 911!?" The kids snickered.

"That, uh. That was me. It was an accident." The class laughed as I turned crimson again. Great.

"How the hell do you '*accidentally*' dial 911?" the SRO barked.

"I was trying to call the front office."

"AND YOU THOUGHT 911 WAS THE BEST WAY TO DO IT!?"

"I mean, the extension *is* 91132."

He turned redder than me, and sputtered "YOU HAVE TO DIAL

NINE FIRST!"

"Well I know that *NOW*."

He stared at me, incredulous, breathing heavily.

I didn't know what to do.

"Thank you," my voice cracked. "...Uh, that will be all, then?" I went back to taking attendance.

"WHAT DOES THAT EVEN *MEAN*!? WHO *ACCIDENTALLY* CALLS 911..." he trailed off, grumbling to himself, as he slammed the classroom door behind him.

Against all odds, the rest of that period went swimmingly. I began to relax, and started to hit my stride. It couldn't possibly get any worse, right? Before I knew it, the bell rang and the second period students arrived.

Now, just as an aside, I was never what you would call a "good" student; I'm pretty sure I was a pain in the ass. I had a comeback for everything, and I was a frequent flier to the principal's office; I was in detention weekly and occasionally on Saturdays. I've seen it all, I've done it all, and by the time I graduated high school, I pretty much had my letterman's jacket in flagrant jackassery.

Before I had even gotten the directions out, I had FOUR kids raise their hands, giggling.

"Yes?"

The girl pointed at her neighbor excitedly, "we already have *all* of our work done."

"Awesome! Can you show me?"

"Uh. *No*. 'Cause it's at home. But since we're done, We're just gonna..." she waved her phone at me.

"Yeah, me too," someone piped up from behind her.

"Same!" another voice called out, which led to more giggles.

It's worth noting that the teacher's original plan was to have them watch videos and take notes on the events. But since the majority of the class suddenly "already had it done," I had them write essays instead.

In art class.

"*In 3 to 5 paragraphs*," my dry-erase marker squeaked off the whiteboard, "*describe your plans after senior year. When you're finished, show me your work and I'll help you edit it.*"

The class groaned, but everyone took out their notebooks. Great!

Everyone *except* the girl who spoke up at the beginning of class.

"I don't know what I'm going to do after high school. So I'm not gonna do this. I'm just gonna, y'know?" She waved her phone at me again.

"Ok well..." I racked my brain "why don't you write about something you *do* know about?"

Her eyes lit up. "Oooh! Like my ex-boyfriend!?"

"Sure." What could *possibly* go wrong with that?

She took a deep breath and rolled her eyes exaggeratedly. "Good, because my *boyfriend* Chad, is like, a total dick. No wait. He's a stupid, *tiny-dicked* dick, and he's my EX-boyfriend, and he *broked* up with me, 'cause he slept over at another girl's house. *AND* he said she's like way better and I feel that I shouldn't have to do work on accounting of all my, uh, heartburn."[2] The class tittered.

I struggled to decode what she just said. "Heartburn? Sure. Great. Write about your heartburn. But try to use professional language, ok?"

As I walked around the room to check on their progress, I had a kid show up late. In the process of putting his late slip on my desk, he "accidentally" knocked over a stack of books, much to the delight of the other students. When I stood up to check on him, he waved his hand dismissively.

"You can just sit back down."

I made a show of adjusting my hearing aid. "I'm sorry, *what*?"

"I *said* you can stay up there. SIT. DOWN." He smirked at me, "*or else.*"

The class went silent, and I'm pretty sure they could hear my heart jackhammering through my chest.

"...Or else *what*?"

"Just, like *or else*, yo." The kids snickered again.

I closed my notebook, and placed it carefully on the desk.

"No....No, my dear boy, you can't just say 'or else.' You *need* to follow it up with something. As in 'sit down, or else I'll *pout aggressively*.' Or maybe 'sit down or else I'll *stomp my feet and cry like a baby*.'"

More laughter from the class.

"What, no! I ain't no baby! Fuck *that*!"

"I didn't say you were. Just relax. You're doing great, buddy!" I gave him a cheery thumbs up.

He thought about it for a second, then looked around the room. "Yeah, how 'bout 'sit down else I blast you in the fuckin' mouth?' *That* would help me relax."

I pretended to think deeply. "Definitely not something I'd recommend." The class went silent.

"Oh yeah? 'Cause I *could!*"

"Indeed you could. The day is positively *brimming* with limitless possibilities."

"Yeah, so...like...yeah!" He deflated visibly when he realized I wasn't going to fight him.

I took off my glasses and cleared my throat. "So, just to be clear, you were just threatening to hit me, right?"

"Yeah."

"You" I pointed at him, "were threatening violence on a teacher." I tapped my pen on the desk, punctuating each word. "You. Threatened. Me."

"Yea...wait. Naw. It's like you said." The realization slowly dawned on him. "No! I was just *exampling the limited possible.* You know?" His voice cracked on the 'know,' and his face reddened more. He sat down, scowling at his phone.

I decided not to push it. The rest of the day went off without incident.

As I drove home, I thought, hey, barring a couple of hiccups, this was manageable! Plus, if every day is like this one, I'll definitely get some great story fodder out of subbing, right?

Somewhere, a single finger of a desiccated monkey fist closed.

February 9th, 2012:

"The tribe has spoken"

So I had one of the best subbing days ever! I "taught" band/instrumental. And by "taught," I mean "commanded an army of band geeks and had them channel my will."

So these non band dingbats came in during lunch being all loud, like "we totally run this room," and the orchestra nerds all stood up, and one yelled "YOU BOW YOUR HEAD IN THE FACE OF GREATNESS! YOU SHOULD KNEEL BEFORE MR. SHAW!

The "swagger mouthy" kids looked at me all incredulously, like "aren't you gonna do something!?"

I shrugged and said "Apparently the tribe has spoken. Looks like you eat your lunch outside, alone."

I got a round of applause. It was glorious.

No shit. It happened.

Oh, and after I said one of my favorite bands is the Foo Fighters, the Jazz club played a stunning 20s style rendition of Everlong on piano, with an accompaniment from an upright bass and drums.

And the kids all want me to sub whenever their teacher is out, and wrote notes to her saying as much. It was fantastic.

Chapter 3:

"Lil' Shaw-Shanked"

The following Monday, my phone rang at 6:17 a.m., but I was ready. The automated system asked whether I wanted to be considered for a sub assignment, and told me that the school was less than three miles from my house! Jackpot! The only thing I didn't really understand was the acronym attached to the class. "ASSIGNMENT 06543. ASPIRATIONS ACADEMY. 1107 PEARSON AVENUE. ROOM SIX. FROM 7:50 A.M. TO 3:30 P.M. TEACHER: BELLSON. S.E.D." Over the next couple of years, I would hear the same automated request weekly.

I excitedly showered, shaved, brushed my teeth, put a little pomade in my hair and dressed in my best button-down plaid shirt. If I could lock down this school as their main substitute, I'd have a four-minute daily commute! I grabbed my coffee and lunch and jumped into the car, practically whistling at my incredible luck.

Even though I had a general idea of where Aspirations Academy was located (based solely on the street name), I still plugged it into Google maps. Only three miles away, and I know the shops around that area. It should be a snap!

I must have driven past the site at least four times. This was supposed to be a school, right? There should be playground equipment, a big parking lot, and big glass windows? At least a lunch-type area, right? Nope. There was just a tiny 10-car lot, in front of a sand-colored building with privacy film over the windows in the middle of a sun-bleached industrial complex.

I knocked on the massive, windowless steel door marked 1107. No answer. There was a rolling gate next to the door, with plastic strips interwoven through the fencing. I couldn't see through it, but I thought I heard kids' voices on the other side.

"Good morning!" I called out. "Is this Aspirations Academy?"

"DEPENDS. WHO ARE YOU?" The voice was loud and curt, almost militaristic. "Yeah, uh. I'm Mac Shaw. I'm here to cover for Ms. Bellson? Uh...S.E.D.?"

"JUST HOLD ON A MINUTE! I'LL WALKIE TARYN TO BUZZ YOU IN."

Seconds later, the steel door buzzed loudly, and I walked into a small, air-conditioned office that was brimming with plants and aromatherapy diffusers. A petite, seemingly ageless Italian woman rushed from around the desk and clasped my hands excitedly.

"Oh you must be MacArthur! We're so happy you were able to take the job! Welcome! Welcome! Why don't you get yourself some coffee! There's a Keurig over there and some doughnuts!" She retreated back behind the desk and began putting a folder together.

To paint a picture, Taryn was that friend's mom that you adored as a kid: she has a warm demeanor and energetic charm that made you want to agree with anything she said. Her voice was cheery, like the tinkling of bells; it made you believe that everything would be just *ducky.*

She pushed the folder into my hands and plopped the key on top of it. "You'll want to keep the stretchy keyring on your arm at all times: it unlocks the office door, the bathrooms, and all classroom doors. Oh! And don't forget your radio, hon!"

I leafed through the folder, nodding along with her. "Ok, I have all the attendance sheets, plus the list of extension numbers. But I still have no idea what S.E.D. stands for. It was on the assignment message that I got."

"Oh! It stands for 'severely emotionally disturbed.' You've worked with special ed before, right?"

"Yes. I taught a mild/moderate class for two months, give or take."

"Oh! Well, you'll be fine then, silly! I think Kelly left the instructions on her desk. If she didn't, just radio me and I'll print more out and send them down! Her room is the last door at the end of the yard. Have a great day and just give me a holler if you need anything!"

Smiling, I walked out of the office into the blazing daylight of the courtyard. As the heavy steel door slammed shut and locked behind me, I realized that I most definitely was *not* in Kansas anymore.

Twelve steel picnic tables were arranged cafeteria style in the main commons, and almost every bench was filled. When the door from the office opened, the yard was buzzing with chatter. When the door slammed behind me, everyone was silent, and all eyes were on me.

As far as I could see, there wasn't a single teacher in sight. The only "true" adult I could see was a "take no shit" 50-something, bald-headed mustachioed black dude who was straight out of an 80s boot camp training montage. He stared at me warily, eyes narrowed, chrome whistle clenched in his teeth.

The students were probably split 90/10 male to female, and of the 40ish students I could see, maybe 5 were white. The rest of the student body, staff and paraprofessionals were people of color, wearing jeans and t-shirts, and I felt like Barney Fife with my too-starched gingham shirt and pressed khakis. To say I looked out of place would have been a gross understatement.

"ALRIGHT EVERYBODY! BREAKFAST IS OVER! GET TO CLASS!" Mr. Drill Sergeant barked this to everyone in earshot, and punctuated it with a long blast from his whistle. All at once, the kids stood, tossed their garbage into the nearby cans, and started walking up the aluminum ramps toward the six classrooms.

I headed to the last door at the end of the quad, keys out, shoulders squared, folder in hand. Seconds behind me was an intense, broad-shouldered 20-something guy, looking every bit like the son of Mr. Drill Sergeant.

As he entered the room, he was already barking orders. "ALRIGHT! MS. BELLSON IS OUT TODAY! GRAB YOUR NOTEBOOKS AND YOUR WORKBOOKS OFF YOUR CLASS SHELF. THIS IS YOUR TEACHER FOR TODAY. HE IS WELL AWARE OF WHAT YOU'RE EXPECTED TO DO AND WILL REPORT YOU TO COACH VIA WALKIE IF YOU AREN'T COMPLYING! DO YOU UNDERSTAND?"

The group, all boys, grumbled "yes" in unison. The aide nodded at me, picked up his clipboard and started taking attendance. Without looking up, he said "I'm David."

"Oh ok. Nice to meet you, David. Ummm. What should I be doing?"

He tossed the clipboard down onto the desk. "Don't even worry about it. We do 90% of the lifting. They just need a credentialed teacher to be in front of the room. Y'know? For legal purposes."

I nodded. "Ok. Well, I'm happy to do whatever. Just let me know."

"Shit, that's new. Most of the other subs are grumpy old men that just do crossword puzzles or read the paper. They don't like to get involved in much of anything."

"Is that what you'd prefer? I'd *love* to get paid to read the newspaper!"

He smiled. "Honestly? Yes. But I'll let you know if we need anything. For now, you can just set up shop at the desk."

I sat awkwardly at the desk in the back of the room, watching David explain the day's plan. He was loud, direct and didn't take any shit from the kids. But there was definitely an unspoken respect between him and the class, and by the third period, they were all joking and laughing...but still managing to get their work done.

At lunchtime, I checked in with the teacher next door. I found the other classroom teachers sitting in the middle of the room, desks circled, chatting about their weekends. They were all exceptionally welcoming and filled me in on the school. Tracy, the older blonde woman, spoke with a kind but firm, matter-of-fact tone. "You know Sagebrush[3]? A lot of these kids were kicked out of there. Or their 'home' school. Most of them have P.O.'s[4], and some live in group homes. Probably like a third or so. For most of 'em, this is the one constant they have each day: two meals, a snack, some exercise and positive relationships with the staff."

Five minutes into the next period, the 80s drill instructor (who all the kids call "Coach") throws the door open, and bellows "ALRIGHT! EVERYONE OUTSIDE SINGLE FILE. YOU ALL KNOW

THE DRILL! NOW!"

As I stand up to leave, David smirks. "You can stay. They're about to bring the dog through."

"Wait. What?" The room was silent.

Seconds later, a police dog and its handler came through the door, sniffing the bookshelves, the couches, the desk, the chairs. Anywhere the kids had access to. I had this moment of actual panic, wondering if it'll smell the joint I smoked two months ago, and how I'm ever going to explain that to the school district. Does weed stay in your clothes like bonfire smoke? No. I'm just being paranoid. *WAIT! Am I high right now!?*

The dog was wholly disinterested with David and I, and made a beeline toward a canvas Jansport bag under one of the desks. The officer grabbed the backpack and left. When the students filed back into the room, I noticed we had one less kid. Nobody seemed surprised.

At the end of the day, as David ushered the kids out into the quad, Jeff, a student that had been in four of the periods I taught, was dragging his feet on his way out. As he shoved his notebook into the bookshelf by the door, he looked at me, then gazed at the board as if lost in thought.

"Y'know Mr. Shaw? You're ok. I actually really like you as a teacher here. You think you're gonna come back?"

Without giving it much thought, I shrugged and said "Sure, Jeff. If they ask me again, I'll be back."

He smiled. "Good, cause I love you man!" He reached into his jacket's inner pocket, fumbling for something.

"Uh. *Thanks*?"

He continued, voice trembling. "I love you so much...that I think

I need to *stab* you!"

Without warning, he lunged at me, pulling something out of his jacket, and shoved it towards my chest. *Hard.*

I didn't even have time to scream (thank God, because it most likely would have come out as a screech). Instead, my brain snapped into old fencing footwork drills (thanks, Mark!) and I compassed backward, rotating 90 degrees on the ball of my foot, allowing him to connect with my shoulder, but pass through the area where I was standing, and continue face first down to the floor.

The weapon? A mashed-up, dirty ski glove.

Jeff cackled madly, jumped to his feet and ran out the door.

I took a deep, shaking breath. I legitimately almost shit myself.

When I turned in the keys at the end of the day, I told Taryn about what had happened. "Oh yeah," she laughed, "that's pretty much daily with Jeff, actually. Did he freak you out? Or do you think you might come back?" She stared at me, smiling expectantly.

Before logic could drip into my brain, I blurted "I mean…if you have more openings?"

"ALL THE TIME!" Taryn purred. "I'll put you on our preferred list right now!"

Two days later, I got a call from Taryn at 6:30 a.m. "Good morning, Mac! Before I put it in the system, I just wanted to see if you'd be interested in covering for Ms. Bellson again?"

"Sure! Same time as before?"

"Yup! Same bat-time, same bat-channel!"

Same classroom, with the same group of kids and the same class aide, David. I filled him in on the "stabbing" story from earlier on in the week, and he laughed.

"Yeah, that pretty much means he likes you." As if on cue, Jeff walked in and gave me a hard high five that left my hand stinging. He fist-bumped David respectfully, with far less force.

"If he didn't like you, I bet you probably wouldn't have come back." David grinned widely. "Believe it or not, Jeff is one of the big movers here. Just--whatever you do--don't ask him for a nickname."

Halfway across the classroom, Jeff's ears pricked up and he swiveled around in his seat to stare at me.

"Oh! So this fool wants a nickname, huh? I mean, he's only been working here a couple days, but lemme see what I can come up with." He mimed cracking his knuckles. David gave me the "oh shit, sorry man" elevator smile, as Jeff shook his hands out.

Not really knowing what to do, I shrugged and managed a weak smile. "Sure. Why not?"

Jeff stood up and circled me, looking me up and down with an exaggerated flourish. "Well, he didn't cry when I lunged at him. That's something. He's white, so it can't be a *cool* nickname, though. Sorry, that's just how it is." He jabbed a finger at my chin. "Shit, that *is* a solid beard, though. Hmmm. How 'bout...Beardman?" He stroked his nonexistent beard, in mock contemplation as the other kids in class laughed. "Yup! That's *definitely* what we gonna call you: BEARDMAN." He glanced at David, smirking. "It's still a fuckload better than Dickface though, huh?"

The rest of the class who watched this exchange expectantly, howled with laughter. Even David rubbed at his mouth, hiding a grin.

Now with the complete attention of the room, Jeff threw open the classroom door and yelled "ayy-YOO!" and his voice reverberated around the quad. Nearby, a school aide sat alongside another group of students; he was a 20-something, gangly white guy that looked like the human version of the 80s animated Ichabod Crane.[5]

"LISTEN UP! FROM NOW ON, THIS FUCKER HERE IS BEARDMAN!" crowed Jeff, as he pointed at me, wild-eyed and grinning. "WHICH IS A WAYYYYYYYYY BETTER NICKNAME THAN DICKFACE...RIGHT, DICKFACE!?"

The group of students out in the quad hooted and laughed, pointing at the now red-faced Ichabod and chanted *"Diiiiick FACE! Diiiiiiiick FACE! DIIIIIIICK FAAAAAAACE!"* as he scowled at them from the benches.

By lunchtime, nearly *every* student was calling me "Beardman" or "Beard-o," thinking that it was a putdown. But I was stoked. *I had a nickname.* And not a terrible one, comparatively speaking!

Over the next five or so years, I subbed at Aspirations for a variety of classes, and was even in line to become a teacher at one point. I did a long-term stint there for three months, and prior to that, I must have taught at that location no less than thirty times. Later on, it became known as "Lil' Shawshank" after I had a class read Stephen King's "Rita Hayworth and the Shawshank Redemption" as our modern novel. But I'm getting ahead of myself.

Even though I began my teaching journey in Scout's classroom, I truly got a crash course in modern education while teaching at Aspirations: I learned that everything stems from genuine relationship building, regardless of how much you know about a topic.

I learned that kids see right through your bullshit, and if you try to fake them out by being something you're not, you'll get a nickname like Dickface...and it'll stick.

I learned to not compare myself to a student's challenges to help get through to them. Sometimes you just need to listen.

But most importantly, I learned that patience and honesty *is* the best policy...especially with kids who had seen darker shit in their first 15 years of life than I had in 34.

I also learned to dodge heckling like a pro...and sling a little back. But more on that later.

October 3rd, 2013:

"Down on the farm"

So, today I was doing my daily "you don't want to be here; elevate yourself" speech, coupled with "you don't want to be a product of your environment… you want your environment to be a product of you" missive from The Departed, in hopes that the kids who are bragging about being pseudo gangbangers might take a cue from me.

One of my outspoken students, Damar, immediately countered "well what do you know about us?"

So I took a deep breath, like always, and shared.

"You kids out here have it lucky in pre juvie! Out here, you get to go on field trips, get two solid meals and snacks! Of all the states I've been through, Iowa has unequivocally the laxest juvie program I've ever seen!

See, back when I was living in Pennsylvania, you had the option of spending one month on a work release, which would equate to three months served in juvie. The only thing was, you had to keep yourself on the up and up; if you got kicked from the work release program, they added between 1 and 4 additional months to your stint, depending on the offense."

I had their undivided attention. Fantastic.

"When I was a teenager, my program was called Farmstead: basically, you spent a month on a farm and had to work from 4:30 a.m. to 4:30 p.m. Monday through Saturday, with a half day on Sunday on account of church and all.

Newbies had to spend their first week cleaning out the chicken coops (which wasn't anything you'd ever wanna do for more than an hour), and if you kept your head down and did your work, you'd get to move upward.

Well, I didn't bother trying to sneak cigarettes (or anything else, for that matter), and kept to myself mostly, spending more time reading in the bunks than risking getting into trouble. And before I knew it, I went from slopping the hogs, to mucking the pens, and by the end of the second week, I got to work in the stables!

Stable work wasn't necessarily easy, but it was kind of like the zen of farm work: you'd change out the straw in the pens, fill the feed cages with hay and keep the water in their basin clean. And, the biggest bonus: being in the barn meant we were working in the shade! Sure, there was the horse crap, but it was nothing close to working in the hog pens! Plus, we'd brush down the horses after they went out to the practice round, and keep their manes and tails free of burrs.

Midway into my third week, the owners purchased three new horses: a big, angry Clydesdale looking monster we called 'Beast,' a jittery Arabian that we called 'Shivers' and a young, messy mare that we called 'Dirty,' on account of all the burrs, mud and dust she'd pick up. 'Dirty' had by FAR the sweetest temperament of the new horses, so I'd spend extra time brushing her down.

Now, I ought to mention that even though the main guy, Mr. Stevens, was impressed with my work, his wife was always giving me a stink eye. It was annoying, because I always minded my language, got my chores finished early and was arguably the best 'employee' they had. But it didn't matter to Mrs. Stevens: she was always screeching 'don't let me catch you on those horses! Just stick to your work!'

Day after day, it was always the same thing. But the kicker was they always kept the saddles under lock and key...and I never learned how to ride using just the mane. So it's not like I ever could have gotten away with it.

So anyway, one afternoon, Ron (another stable worker) and I were taking Dirty and Kelly (one of the older mares) out to the paddock where they could walk around on their own. After brushing them and giving them some 'snack oats,' we put them in the far paddock and were about to head back. But Ron noticed two big tractor tires just past the rails, near the big, unmown hill at the back behind the barn.

'We got finished early,' he said 'wanna race tires!?'

After all the work I'd put in that day, barreling down the hill in those tractor tires seemed like fun, so I looked back towards the porch where sour old Mrs. Stevens was usually glaring at me. Nothing.

As I checked my tire for spiders (couldn't be too

careful), Ron just went full bore down the hill, laughing like a madman.

I set up my tire, and started the topsy turvy descent.

I gained a little speed, but wobbled out, landing on my side, halfway down the hill. Ron made it all the way to the bottom.

And as I was brushing the dirt off my arms, ready to go back down, I heard a shrill whistle from the farmhouse.

When I turned around, I saw Mrs. Stevens on the porch, with a set of binoculars, and I swore that I could see her frown from where I was standing. And she had someone with her. Mr. Stevens.

Shit.

So while Ron got to have all the fun, I got caught… red handed.

They saw me rolling.

And they were hating!

They were patrolling.

'Cause they were trying to catch me ridin' Dirty!"

The classroom exploded with choruses of "OHHHHHHH FUUUUCK OFFFFFFFF" and "NO FUCKIN' WAY!" No overturned desks this time, but they were all smiles.

Totally worth the set up.

And before you doubt it: yes, it happened. Yes, it

was glorious. And Yes. I'll absolutely trick *'em all*
again.

Chapter 4:

"The Stone That Sharpens"

Cutting my teeth at Lil' Shawshank was simultaneously the best and worst possible way for me to experience the full impact of teaching; it was Schrödinger's Classroom.

It was *a lot* like learning to swim by being thrown into the deep end of a lake...that also happened to be crawling with alligators. If you were somehow able to survive, everything else was cake.

In a lot of ways, substituting was like being an opener at a comedy club--or worse, a middler at a coffee shop's community open mic night. The year prior, I had dabbled in stand-up comedy at open mics with some friends, and had even done a few opener gigs at local clubs. In both subbing and stand-up, you have to make sure that the crowd is "with you" from the start, and somehow manage to keep them with you for the entirety of your time. But more than anything, you *have* to go into it expecting to get heckled; it's when you think that you're completely in control that you absolutely are *NOT*.

Like a comic, you try to anticipate crowd response and potential for heckling moments, and you keep some jokes in your pocket *specifically* for those instances. Lil' Shawshank kept me fresh and punchy when it came to comebacks, especially during the early years. Working with the S.E.D. population was great, because they rarely took things seriously, and would give you props when a joke landed. Those classrooms were typically loud, rowdy and energetic, and it got to the point where I didn't even really need to bring coffee to work every day, because the potential for disaster was more than enough to keep me awake and on my toes, both mentally and physically.

As an outsider, getting to watch the interactions between staff and students was incredible; I had come from a school that was never condescending to kids, but it also wasn't exactly speaking to them on their level either. Scout's school had a *very* distinct line between staff and students (thanks to a couple of *major* misconduct allegations in years past), and that had directly affected the student/staff relationship building.

At Lil' Shawshank, the staff spoke to the kids directly and bluntly, and any sarcasm had the undercurrent of caring and respect. "You *need* to chill a little more," "that sounds *a LOT* like bullshit, to be honest," and "knock that shit off!" were all tossed around daily, both from the aides and the students themselves. From the staff, words were never wielded as weapons; rather a way to speak to the kids in a tone that they were familiar with. Saying something like "well Richie, I think that you should use better choices" would elicit an instant eye roll and double middle fingers--whereas saying something like "Richie, what the *hell* did you think was gonna happen?" would get you an honest and thoughtful response.

Getting to the place where I could balance sass with meaningful teaching took more than a year, and there were many learning opportunities during that time. The biggest lesson I learned was that you couldn't rush relationship building...*especially* at that school.

When I first got to Aspirations, I marveled at the fluidity of communication between the staff and students. Unfortunately, every time I tried to engage them, I felt like I was coming across as hokey and pandering--like Dickface the "try hard."[6] I would watch the interactions that teachers had with not only the students, but the staff and each other as well, and I wanted it too. Here was an amazing, direct, no frills, no *bullshit* way of communicating in a school that was pure and genuine. In a lot of ways, it's where my current teaching style was born.

Early on, I erred on the side of caution and tried to observe as much as possible. During my tenth (or so) time that I taught there, I got caught up in the ease of communication, and tried to talk to the kids like the staff did. What I failed to realize was that the ease of communication came with years of relationship building and trust. And subbing six times a month was no replacement for staff and teachers that had been with them for years. Those of you who know me are painfully aware that listening isn't exactly my strong suit, but after a couple of foot-in-mouth moments, I decided to try to be more of an active listener.

It was my 15th time covering Ms. Bellson, and I was getting along better with the kids and staff. Unfortunately, on that day, half the school's staff were sick, which meant minimal support presence. On the upside, of the five present support staff, two were 6'5", 300+ pound twin brothers, one of whom was an ex-left tackle from Iowa State. I also had David, "Coach" and Lil' Shawshank's surly assistant coach, Matt. This was during the height of flag football season, and the kids all knew that acting up during the school day would mean extra punishing practices--usually line drills followed by windsprints (aka "suicides") with a generous pile of BTP's--Burpees Til (you) Puke.

I was covering Bellson's English class all day, and the agenda had only four items:

- Vocabulary (*prodigious, spectacles, durable, sustained, synthesis, exalted* and *vibrant*): write 5 sentences using the vocabulary words in the word bank.

- Holiday vacation paragraph (5+ SENTENCES! NO COPYING!)

- Community service essay topic sentence.

- Fill out your research project outline.

Of course, in her notes she also said *"you'll be lucky if you get them to complete a single assignment, so don't stress."*

Challenge accepted.

One of the main reasons I got along so well with both the staff and the students, was that I hardly ever took anything too seriously. So for the first 10 minutes or so, I knew to expect "fuck you, I ain't doing shit," or some combination of slurs and profanity bracketing a similar message. Once they noticed that nobody was paying attention to them, they would try a last ditch negative attention dive: throwing something, yelling something, flipping me off, etc.

When I didn't respond, they usually got bored and got their work out.

I often used this specific tactic with students prone to violent escalation--letting them blow off verbal steam cleared the way for them to work, and added a little levity to the room. Later, I could check in when they didn't have as attentive of an audience.

It's silly, but 90% of the time, the *"you hungry?"* approach usually worked. Whenever someone was acting out, I'd pull them aside after they finished posturing, and would offer something from my bag of tricks: a breakfast bar or those crumbly granola bars in the green package almost always worked. Even if you're not hungry, who's really going to pass up a pre-packaged snacky-snack that they could trade to someone later?

Of course, it didn't hurt that I also made side deals with the students on top of that. For example, if they could go 20 minutes without cussing, they earn extra "dollars" which they can use to buy a packet of peanut butter crackers, granola or fruit snacks from the canteen. In particularly rough classrooms, I'd have a list of stacks on the board: 10 minutes without profanity = 1.5x bonus. 20 minutes = 2x bonus, 30 = 2.5x, etc. And if they somehow go a whole period without a violent outburst, they get to pick the rec time game for their table during break–which only happened once or twice per week.

On this particular day, Richie and Shawna managed to go the entire period without cussing *or* slap-boxing, which was highly unusual. Just as the bell was about to ring, Shawna calls Richie "a bitch ass ginger leprechaun."

Everyone heard her, so Richie (a diminutive, painfully pale red-headed kid) who said nearly *everything* in black slang, was the "no cuss" winner for the day, which was pretty impressive. He chose dominoes for his table's lunch activity, and the other kids in class agreed with his choice. Smooth sailing.

Shawna wasn't even mad about losing. "I fucked it up for myself," she shrugged as she was putting her folder away. "I'm still gonna wreck him in dominoes though!"

As the lunch bell rang, I thought to myself: *is it possible? Is this going to be my perfect game? The mythical sub version of a "no-hitter?" A day where no dreams would die?*

Spoiler alert: it wasn't.

Before leaving the room, Shawna brought her classwork over to me.

"Hey Shaw? If I finish this shit up during lunch, will I still get my $40 bonus for completing two assignments?"

Technically, she shouldn't have. But Shawna was on an uncharacteristic roll this week, and was intensely self-motivated to rack up bonus dollars wherever she could.

"Sure, Shawna. Just make sure you get it back to me before rec is over, or else no bonus, ok?"

"Yup! Thanks!" She darted out of the room and stomped down the ramp to join the lunch line.

I should probably clarify: we didn't *actually* give our students cash--we would give the students laminated fake money when they're working especially hard, and they could use those "dollars" to rent MP3 players, extra pillows for the couch (which some rooms had), extra bathroom passes, chips, etc. The "A-Bucks" were an excellent incentive for students who were on the fence as to how they were going to behave that day. Plus, it wasn't bribery so much as it was payment for services rendered; the service in this case was not giving me any additional headaches.

I checked over Shawna's paper and noticed she had three sentences from the word bank written down. Considering she already did the second assignment, this extra assignment was gravy, and would get her additional bonus bucks. Smart.

After I had finished my lunch, I decided to take a lap around the quad. But really? I wanted to check on their domino game. I strolled up just as Shawna put down a double six and nabbed herself a clean 25 points, which prompted instant complaining from Richie. Having none of it, Shawna threw a hard middle finger in his face "Bam! 25 says fuck you leprechaun! Go cry into your Lucky Charms!"

The table laughed, as Ritchie scowled. Without warning, he snorted, reared back his head...and hocked a loogie at Shawna.

Time seemed to freeze. Not only was this completely out of nowhere, but he did it with such an exaggerated motion that I don't even think Shawna flinched; almost like she was thinking "no WAY someone's dumb enough to do that in real life."

Thankfully, his spitting aim was as good as his domino skills, so a clump of spit and slimy snot hit her arm...and not her face.

I watched Shawna's eyes widen in rage, and she stood up, scraping the runner of snot and spit off her arm with the heel of her palm. *Hurk.* I could feel the chewed-up sandwich I had just finished rise to the back of my throat.

I was mid-way through roaring "RICHIE! GET TO THE OFFICE!" when Shawna narrowed her eyes, and tilted her head at him like Michael Myers.

Oh. Oh *no.*

As she loomed over him, Richie remained sitting and grinned up at her, his posture effectively saying "we both know you ain't gonna do shit." After she scraped the snot streak off her arm, she used that *same* hand to return it back to Richie...via slap.

Now, when I say that this slap was the slap to end *all* slaps, believe me; it deserved a slo-mo, SportsCenter-level breakdown.

As it impacted, Shawna actually leaned into it, rolling her shoulder and adding extra force to the already vicious (and *viscous*) downward arc. The impact was even louder, given the wetness of her hand--it sounded like someone had shot off a firecracker.

The silence that followed was deafening.

Richie's tiny frame wasn't built to support such an impact, and when his face rocked to the left, his body had no choice but to follow suit. Unfortunately for him, his legs were tucked under the bench he was sitting on, and the tiny red-headed Tower of Babel went crashing down.

I ran around to check on Richie as two aides closed on Shawna, and he was still sprawled out on the ground, legs tangled comically around the bench, literally stunned. His eyes watered, and a giant red handprint rose on his cheek, with his own snot matting his sideburns and eyebrow. *Hurk.* Oh no. Here comes the sandwich again. A crowd had gathered around the table.

The rest of the quad exploded with a chorus of "*OOOOOOOOOOOOOOOOOHHHHHHHH!*"

When I turned towards Shawna, she put both of her hands up and frowned. "I lost my temper and shouldn't have hit him. Fuck. *FuuuuuuUUCK!*"

As one of the aides escorted her towards the office, she called out to Richie, loud enough for all to hear:

"That *prodigious* slap that you sustained left a *vibrant* handprint on your face, bitch!"

The quad roared again, and Shawna turned back to me, deadly serious.

"I just did a sentence, but I used more than two bonus words. I still get my extra $10, right?"

I nodded at her, and she grinned.

She may have gotten a 3-day suspension, but she came back with an extra $20 in her account; $10 for the vocab words, and another $10 for the show.

After I had been subbing there regularly for a couple of months, Richie decided to get the attention of all the kids in class by shit-talking me mid-way through attendance.

"Yo! Fatbeard! I seent you pull in today in yo lil' green car this morning."

"Did you now?" I kept taking roll, silently checking names off.

"Yuuuuuuuuuup. You know your car makes you look like a f*ggot, right?"

The class hushed, and a few kids laughed, covering their mouths. I looked up from my clipboard.

"You know, Richie, if I had a dollar for every time I heard that…"

"…You'd have like a thousand dollars, huh!?" He sat back and grinned broadly as the kids around him slapped him on the shoulders, laughing.

"No, Richie. I'd have closer to four thousand. And that *still* wouldn't be enough to buy my husband the vacation he *truly* deserves."

The class fell silent, and Richie's eyes got huge as he started to sputter excuses.

"Yo…*naw*…like, look. I didn't know. I mean. Uh. I didn't even mean it like *that*. For REAL! I was just…"

"You were *just* using hate speech as a punchline?" He stared back at me, face red and eyes wide, seemingly on the verge of tears. It was as if all of the air was taken out of the room, and nobody said a word.

"We'll talk about it later. Ok everyone, take out your copy of 'There Will Come Soft Rains.' Who can tell me where we left off yesterday?" Class resumed, all except for Ritchie who stared at me with huge eyes all period.

Later on at lunch, Richie came into the classroom with his head down. "I didn't mean to disrespect you or your man. I swear."

I put my sandwich down. "Richie. I'm not gay." His eyes narrowed at me, and seconds later he exploded, waving his arms around.

"YO DUDE WHAT THE FUUUUUUUCK!?"

"...But imagine if I had been." He stopped pacing. "If I *was* gay...or if other people in this class were, how do you think they'd feel?"

"But you *know* I was joking, though!"

"Sure, and: what if someone in class, a friend of yours, was *this close* to coming out to you? *This close* to trusting you with their real self? But then they heard you use them as a punchline. You think they'd still trust you with that information?"

"*Fuck* no. But look, I'm not tryin' to date any dudes here..."

"No, Richie. You're missing my point: the words you use have weight. And if you're using terms that are considered hate speech and they get reported, how do you think your P.O. is gonna take that? I'm not looking for an answer. Just think about it. Now if you wouldn't mind? I'd like to finish my lunch."

He headed back out to the quad, chewing on his lip, deep in thought. At least, that's what I wanted to believe.

Sadly, that wasn't the last "serious" conversation I had with Richie over my three years at Lil' Shawshank; he was what Charlie Murphy referred to as "*a habitual line stepper*" and needed to be checked, corralled and redirected daily.

One of the last conversations I ever had with him made him cry. Like many of the students at Lil' Shawshank, Richie's family didn't have a whole lot of money, and he had it in his mind that he would become a Soundcloud rapper as a career. I had told him months before that I would buy him a "good" journal to write his raps down in, since all of his verses were written on scraps of paper, which he was prone to losing. And as obnoxious as he could be, Richie actually had pretty good rhyme skills. So I picked up one of those journals that have a loop attached for a pen (since he was continually losing pens too), and brought it on the last day I was teaching at Aspirations. He actually teared up and said "lots of people promise me shit, but nobody ever has followed through. You're a real one."

As he took the notebook from me, I couldn't help but smile. Not because I did a good thing, or whatever good deed positive karmic bullshit I was now a part of. No, I was smiling because on the last page of the journal, I wrote *"by accepting this journal, I, Richie Marshall, agree to give MacArthur C. Shaw 40% of all future earnings from my recording career."*

I'm *sure* it'll stand up in court.

One afternoon, as the students piled in from lunch, Kellie (an outspoken protest-addict), had the class iPad playing the PETA "Killing Dogs Fur Farm" viral video that had been making the rounds on social media. It was an insanely graphic video showing footage of a Chinese fur farm, with shrieking dogs getting slaughtered by apathetic workers. I didn't have to see the video to know what it was, because those screeches were haunting, and stuck with me long after watching it.

After half the class was fully grossed out, Kellie approached my desk, and proudly displayed it to me:

"ISN'T THAT DISGUSTING, MR. SHAW?!?"

I winced visibly. "That's messed up, Kellie. Really messed up."

The kids all snickered, thinking that they managed to gross me out immediately after lunch. Kellie was beaming.

"It's really messed up, Kellie, 'cause I just finished eating…"

What started as a low chuckle was slowly getting louder, as she stomped a victory lap around the room.

I locked eyes with her, and grinned. "…and now I'm hungry again."

The laughter ceased. Kellie frowned deeply, and feigned vomiting sounds.

"Now, unless anyone has any take-out from whatever restaurant that *amazing* commercial is from, we should begin…"

"*EWWWWWWWWWWWWW!*"

After four months at Aspirations, I think I saw more fistfights on school property than I had in my entire life up to that point. Cut in line? Fistfight. Trip someone during a pickup game of basketball? Fistfight. Buy the last Flamin' Hot Cheetos from the canteen? Fistfight. The wildest thing to me was that it was almost always the new kids that would scrap (or initiate a scrap), while the "kings" would hang back and observe; it was like the creed of every cable TV prison show: pick a fight on your first day in to establish to the rest of the block that you aren't weak.

It's probably going to come across as decidedly un-P.C., but I believe that there's something to be learned from getting punched in the face really, *really* hard after running your mouth: you learn that actions have consequences and (hopefully) that getting punched in the face really isn't something you want to make a habit of.

When I was a kid, I had said something along the lines of "yeah, just like I did your mom" to a classmate named Jerry that was talking shit to me. *BAM*. I got punched in the face so hard that I couldn't see out of my left eye for a few seconds. Everything was fuzzy with static, and my nose felt like it was humming That would have been a prime opportunity for Jerry to throw a second punch ...but he didn't. He just glared at me, and quietly said "my mom died last year."

Did I learn from that adventure? You bet your ass I did: from that day on, I wouldn't insult anyone's mother if I hadn't met them before. Because you *never* know...and I didn't much feel like getting punched in the face again.

As much as we're supposed to remain steadfast against them, every teacher smiles a little inside when an obnoxious kid gets smacked hard for talking shit to someone he shouldn't have. I'm not talking about a "hold him down and hit him with a sock full of quarters" beating; I mean more like the lesson Jerry taught me in fifth grade: If you are blatantly asking for an ass-kicking, you shouldn't be surprised when it happens.

On this particular morning, there only minor dust-ups, and all of the kids had managed to complete their work with the normal amount of prompting. The day dragged a little, but we got all of our work done by lunchtime.

The afternoon class was a completely different bunch, and their lunch buzz had worn off considerably, which *should* have meant they were ready to work--or ready to *fake* the fact that they're working--both of which I rewarded. After all, if I couldn't make them better students, I *would* make them better liars...and both of those traits could help them succeed in the real world.

Instead, Trevor, the diminutive "wide receiver" for the school's fledgling flag football team, and Roger, the 5'5, 250-pound human meatball, were competing for the attention of the only girl in the classroom: the pseudo-skinhead, Vivian.

Usually, I allocate the first 10 minutes of class for shenanigans, but since the afternoon class had slacked off all week, I was at the end of my rope.

"ALLLLLLL RIGHT EVERYBODY! LET'S GET IT TOGETHER, SHALL WE!?" Vivian and the other six students immediately stopped their chatting, and opened their binders. Roger and Trevor? Not so much.

"Look at him up there," Trevor quipped in his prepubescent falsetto lisp, "He think*th* he run this cla*th*."

"Yeah," Roger joined in "He ain't running shit."

They both exploded into high-pitched cackles. I took a deep breath

"Roger? You try too damn hard. Stop it. If you wanted to make a fat joke, you should have followed Trevor's 'he thinks he run this class' with 'naw man, look at him: he hasn't run a day in his life!'" The class did an exaggerated *OOOOHHHHH!* I continued. "Now, if you're done trying to one-up the master, it's time to get your notebooks out."

Roger turned to Trevor for a cue of what to do next. Trevor stared hard at me, eyebrows furrowed, trying to come up with a retort.

Y'see, Roger is one of those guys in high school who can't make his own mind up. He's like the world's worst clout-chasing hypeman: he follows around people higher on the food chain as they trash talk, sneering *"yeah!"* and repeating what someone just said, because he's not clever enough to come up with anything on his own.

Trevor, on the other hand, is a teacher's nightmare because he's an agitator--even if he doesn't believe something, he'll still egg on his subordinates. Plus, he has a Napoleon complex, coupled with a doughy strut and a trilling lisp that makes my brain itch. All of the words in his vocabulary that end in 's' are drawn out *'thhhh'* sounds. And he smacks the top of his desk to punctuate nearly everything he says.

My biggest frustration with Trevor is that he's one of the suburban upper-middle class white kids that uses the word 'n***a,' 'Blood' and 'homie' in damn near every sentence. After, of course, glancing around to make sure that there are no *actual* Bloods around. Most of the other students of color didn't pay him much mind, and actually laughed at him...not *with* him. He was a class pet of sorts, not unlike Ritchie.

"Trevor," I purred *"are we moving on?"*

Trevor didn't reply, but stared at me, squinting hard. I could almost hear the gears in his head cranking to come up with something worse. If he pushed himself any harder, he would likely shit his pants.

"Yeah, well...you...uh...you fat a*th fuck*. You might want to s*thop* eating so your Goodwill clothes fit better."

No reply from the class, except a *"wamp-waaaah"* of failure from someone in the back. Excellent.

"Sure, Trevor. I might try that." I pointed at his track jacket "Hey, speaking of clothes, when did Build-A-Bear start selling Adidas outfits?"

The class snickered, but Trevor hadn't quite caught the joke yet. He was about to fire off another smartass comment, but caught Roger laughing in his peripheral.

"Tha FUCK you laughing at?"

Roger laughed louder. "I'm laughing at YO little teddy bear ass!" Trevor scowled at him.

Now that their alliance was broken, I could sweep in and begin the lecture.

"All right, everyone open your binders to the 'Rome' tab. Who wants to start us off by reading the top part?"

Against all odds, I was able to power through most of the lesson with only minor issues. But then, there was a knock at the door.

Turns out, Matt, another relatively new student, had gotten kicked out of his class, and asked if he could do his homework in my room, since we got along pretty good. Matt was one of the starters on the school's flag football team, and it's probably important to mention: he was also one of the seven black students on campus.

He took a seat at one of the round, satellite tables near the door and started working quietly. The thing I loved about Matt was that he was one of those kids that just keeps his head down and gets shit done...and I respect the hell out of his work ethic. He was also visibly strong, but kept things quiet when it came to trash talk.

The students at Aspirations all carried a card that teachers from each class would fill out at the end of each period, as a way to track their progress throughout the day. Just before the end-of-period bell rang, I told Matt to go back to his previous classroom and get his daily report sheet so I could add positive notes and extra dollars to it. As he left to get his sheet, Trevor was mumbling and giggling to Roger. Never *ever* a good sign.

A few minutes later, I heard a knock at my door, and Trevor sprung up and offered to open it. I was busy filling out the students' cards for the period, so I actually kind of appreciated it. Opening the doors is a daily pain, because the classroom doors were locked from the outside to discourage kids from leaving class to visit their friends, and potentially distract other classes. The teacher's desk tended to be near the back wall of the room, which meant a long walk to open the door every time a student knocked.

Trevor gently opened the door, but as Matt started to pull it the rest of the way open, Trevor instead yanked the handle back hard, which slammed the door, and locked it from the outside. I could hear Matt swearing through the door.

"Oh he *real* mad!" Trevor giggled.

"I would be too," I said. "Now open the door, already."

"Okay!" He began to push it open again. But before Matt could get the door fully open, Trevor yelled "NOPE!" and slammed it again. Great.

"TREVOR!?" I sighed, exasperated. "If I have to…"

"Oh all riiiiigh…" As Trevor went to goose the door open a third time, Matt let out a howl and tore the door open from the outside, dragging Trevor, with his hand firmly on the handle, along with it.

Whoops.

I could hear yelling and chaos from the hall, so I started towards the door, just as Trevor was shoved back inside, screeching.

*"FUUUUUUCK N***A! RELAX MAN! DAMN!"*

Matt charged into the room. "N***a?! *N***A!?!*" He lunged at Trevor, who was just barely able to dance away, yelling in his high-pitched trill "DAMN BITCH! CHILL!"

I picked up the classroom's walkie-talkie and barked. "NEED HELP IN 330, NOW!" In the background, Trevor yelled in his singsong voice. "Yeah! Get this lil' n***a outta here already!"

Apparently that was Matt's breaking point. He ducked down and threw a brutal left hook, smashing his massive fist into the side of Trevor's head. A chorus of "OOOOOOOOOHHHHHHS" went up from the rest of the class.

Damn.

"*AAAAAGHHHHHH! Fuck! FUUUUUCK!*" Trevor lunged backward, clutching his ear...and promptly splayed into a heap on the floor. I couldn't tell whether Trevor tripped over his own feet, or if his two pairs of sagging sweatpants tripped him up.

Trevor curled up on the floor, as Matt straddled his side, ready to rain more punches down on him.

"***THAT'S ENOUGH!***" I roared, as I grabbed Matt and spun him backwards, out of the classroom.

Security met me at the door, and dragged Matt down to the principal's office. By that point, Trevor, tears streaming down his face, was back on his feet and weakly pushing against the aides. "LEMME AT THAT BITCH!" he sniffled. "HE LUCKY THEY HOLDIN' ME BACK!"

This went on for another couple minutes. Trevor kept cry-yelling, even though Matt had long since been hustled to the office.

Eventually, Trevor stopped yelling, and opted instead for clutching his ear and making the "*sssssss! ahhhh!*" pain sounds. Then, his eyes flew open comically.

"My rock! MY FUCKIN' ROCK!" He dove back down on the carpet, pawing the floor. "MY FUCKIN' DIAMOND FELL OUT! MY DIAMOND EARRING FELL OUT! THAT SHIT'S *THO* EXPEN*TH*IVE! IT WAS A RARE DIAMOND! FUCK!"

As he scrambled around on the floor, I walked over to help him out. "What kind of diamond, man?"

"FUCK! IT'S A MOI*TH*UREITE OR *THOMETH*IN'!"

"A *Moistureite*?"

"YEAH! I*TH* A MOI*TH*URITE CAUTH IT'S THE CLEARE*TH*T KIND OF DIAMOND! FUCK!"

Against my better judgment, I grabbed a flashlight to help him look. I had to see this "moisturite" diamond for myself.

Minutes later, Trevor yelled out "AH-HA!" and held the diamond up like it was the Heart of the Ocean.

I squinted at him. "Can I see that?"

It was exactly what I thought it was: one of those gaudy, cut glass cube "diamonds" that they sell at mall kiosks. The guy must have told him it was a Moissanite diamond...but they didn't even bother cutting it into a proper gem shape.

As he jammed the glass cube awkwardly back into his ear, he alternated between hitching sobs and sucking snot back up into his nose.

"He'*th* lucky...*huh huh*...that all tho*the* people...*huuuuuuh*...got in between u*th*."

"Yup. Really lucky, huh?"

"Yuh."

Did he learn anything? Probably not. *Did I learn anything?* Shit yeah I did! I could have make a *fortune* selling teenagers fake diamonds at a mall kiosk instead of subbing!

One afternoon, I decided to eat outside since the weather was nice and the staff mentioned that they were down a person for lunch duty. At Lil' Shawshank, lunch duty usually meant that you kept a general eye on the chaos; whether it was staff joining a pickup basketball game, or using that time to check in with students in a small-group (or one-on-one setting).

Since I was an outlier, I tended to sit on the tables in the outer ring of the quad, which not only gave me a good view of the area, but also allowed me a little quiet time. I hadn't even finished unpacking my lunch bag when Pete, one of the more influential (and total hardass) students, sat down beside me with an exaggerated sigh. He's broad-shouldered and surly, and stands at just under six feet tall. It's a safe bet that he'll be taller than me when he graduates.

Pete (along with two other Senior students), is known as one of Lil' Shawshank's aforementioned "kings" to both students and staff alike. As I mentioned before, there are a select group of students who rule the roost, and it pays to stay on their good side. Plus, it goes without saying, if you have the "kings" on your side, the whole day tended to go a lot smoother. Of course, having *all* the kings on your side at the same time is near impossible. So you have to know how to play their game, and pick and choose which horse to back on each particular day.

Example: Rob, another one of my pain in the ass students, decided that he was going to sprawl across three desks and sleep through class. Unfortunately, I had a lesson planned and needed everyone in their seats and taking notes. The second time I asked

Rob to get off the desks, Pete nodded at Matt, who took it upon himself to grab the back of the seats and angle the desks down… and relocate Rob to the floor.

"MATT!" I had to feign frustration, "that is *not* appropriate!"

The other students hurriedly took out their binders and started copying down the day's notes, as not to invoke the wrath of Matt. In the right situations, it can be quite tidy.

On the flipside, if you end up on the other side of the kings, your work hours will be a living hell. I already told you about Dickface, but I haven't yet mentioned the ballad of Mr. Hopkins. Hop, as the rest of the staff called him, was a first-year academic (read: non-disciplinary) aide in the geology classroom. He was young, smug, and above all, inflexible. Within three days, Shawna (who happened to be another king…or *queen*, if you will) took it upon herself to rechristen him "Shit-lip" on account of his poor attempt at growing a mustache. Three years later (and clean-shaven), he's still greeted with a cheery "hey, Shit-lip!" by nearly every student.

In any case, back to lunch: Pete and I sat watching the pickup basketball game in silence. A couple other kids joined the table and ate silently, occasionally looking at Pete for a cue to say something. After a few minutes, he dropped his Lunchables pack loudly into the paper bag, and turned to me.

"Let me ask you something?"

Keep in mind, this is the first *actual* conversation I've had with Pete; most days he comes to class late, then sits in the back of the room and scowls. He gets all of his work done without a fuss, and whenever I come in to check on him, he completely disregards me, save for a single hand up, as if to say "nope. Not now. Not *ever*."

Now, this lunchtime visit has just turned into an audition.

"Wait," my inner nerd started to panic. *"AM I SITTING AT THE COOL KIDS' TABLE BY DEFAULT NOW?! Be cool. You got this."*

I give him a noncommittal shrug. "Sure, Pete. What's up?"

"You been dating girls and whatnot for awhile, right?" I nodded. "Well, like, how do you know that the girl you're with, like, is any better than the other ones out there?"

I thoughtfully chewed my sandwich. "I don't know, Pete. You just know, I guess. Like, even though I can appreciate another beautiful woman, I've never been happier going home to the one I have."

Pete screwed up his face at me, laughing. "Fuck outta here!"

"No man, it's the truth! And the trick is to find one that digs you for being you. One that accepts your flaws along with your strengths...know what I mean?"

He nodded, and held up his lunch bag. "Ok, check it: my girl knew I was havin' a shit day, right? And she knows that Kit-Kats are my favorite. Well, right before lunch, *someone* dropped off a lunch with Lunchables and two Kit-Kats at the front office. Not those little Halloween Kit-Kats either. I'm talkin' *full-sized Kit-Kats!* Is that like what you're talking about?"

"That depends. If it was your mom that dropped it off, I'd recommend against dating her."

He laughed loudly, which prompted the other kids at the table to chuckle along nervously.

"NAWWWW MAN! No, for real, my girlfriend knew I forgot my lunch today, so she dropped one off for me. Like, I love her and whatever, but what if there's something else better out there?"

"You know, Pete? There's always 'something better' out there. But you need to be happy with what you have. A wise man once said "there's a billion fine-looking women in the world, dude. But they don't all bring you Kit-Kats at school. Most of 'em will just cheat on you."

"Oh word? Thanks Shaw."

"Don't thank me, Pete. Thank Kevin Smith."

"Uh. Ok. Does he teach at another school you work at?"

Now, to me that exchange was a win; without hyperextending myself or bribing Pete with snacks, I was able to start building a better relationship with him. In the weeks following, his entire demeanor shifted during our classroom conversations. I wouldn't say he was necessarily friendly, but he was definitely more attentive.

Months later, when I was waiting to be let in outside the main gate, I saw Trevor lounging at a table nearby. Unprovoked, he points at me and grins "oh good. Thi*th* fat bitch i*th* back."

Before I can even respond, Pete materializes from around a corner, like an angry, Hispanic Batman...complete with a raspy growl.

"*TREVOR!* How you gonna call someone a bitch, when yo lispy, missed-puberty-ass voice sounds like my six-year-old little sister's?"

Trevor whirled around to say something back, until he realized where the jab came from.

"Yeah, well...I. Uh. I, like, was *th*aying thi*th* joke, and..."

"Your dad made a joke when he hatefucked your mom and didn't pull out."

I swear, between "missed-puberty-ass" and "hatefucked your mom," the little teleprompter that had all of my dialogue was blank. No, strike that. It was *unplugged.* I had nothing.

Trevor looks at me, mouth gaping, then back to Pete. "Sin*th* when the fuck do…"

"SINCE WHEN THE FUCK DO I ANSWER YOUR QUESTIONS!?" Pete roared at Trevor, eyes blazing and fists clenched.

Trevor, the very definition of a shivering human Pomeranian, puts his hands up, palms out, with eyes as big and round as saucers. "DAMN Pete, *th*orry! Fuck!"

"Not half as sorry as you're gonna be if you don't bring me some fucking orange juice…"

"*Th-th*ure. Yeah. No problem!" Trevor took off like his shorts were on fire.

Pete pushed the gate open, greeting me with a combination handshake/fist-bump.

"This fuckin' kid, huh?" Pete had massive dark circles under his eyes.

"You good?"

"Yeah man. Quit smoking Tuesday night." He exhaled deeply. It was Thursday morning.

I whistled. "Good for you, bud! How're you holding up?"

"Good. As good as I *can*, anyway. I'll be a lot fucking better when someone *BRINGS ME MY FUCKIN' ORANGE JUICE!*" Pete's roar echoed across the campus.

I heard Trevor yelp something shrill in response.

"SOMETIME TODAY WOULD BE GREAT!"

Pete gives me a *'what are ya gonna do?'* shrug.

"Try not to kill him?"

Pete grinned "Every *single* day."

Trevor jogged up a couple minutes later, breathless, with a carton of orange juice.

Pete looked at him, unblinking. *"Where's. My. Fucking. STRAAAAW!?"*

Trevor's shoulders dropped, and he spun around and sprinted back across campus, puffing like an asthmatic locomotive.

It wasn't uncommon to work a "swing shift" at Lil' Shawshank, which meant I was in multiple classes, covering for teachers who were in meetings, at appointments, or had other things to do. It was nice, because it gave me a compartmentalized cross-section of all of the classrooms in a single day. Plus, the teacher was usually there at the beginning of the day, and almost always came back before I had to leave, so students were less likely to get squirrely. After all, knowing that the Den Mother (or Father) could be lurking just outside the door was usually enough to keep them under control.

Of the *seven* different classrooms at Lil' Shawshank, I saw many of the same students multiple times. In the last class of that day, I saw two students for the *fifth* time; Tucker and Leon.

To put it in perspective, Tucker looks like the ruddy-faced child of Shaggy and Sam Rockwell; he has shifty eyes, a shotgun spray of acne across his face and a sneering way of talking that doesn't win him any points with anyone. Conversely, Leon looks like Ice Cube circa 1997: tall, broad-shouldered and aloof, but occasionally laughs with a booming bark that usually makes everyone around him join in.

Throughout the day, Tucker had been subversively obnoxious, trying to rally the students around him into some sort of single-period rebellion. The thing was, I could smell the sharp tang of "victim" coming off him; he's either getting bullied at school, or is being emotionally pummeled at home...or both. And brother, that stink is coming off him in *waves*. He was looking to assert some kind of dominance over the room, because he's clearly not feeling in control of *his* situation at home.

Meanwhile, most (if not all) of these kids have had me before, so they're aware that there's an expectation of work completion in the class. That being said, it was the last period of the day, and at the end of a long week, *everyone wants a show.*

Up until this point, I had explained the day's assignment and actively ignored Tucker's snide comments, mostly because he was mumbling them under his breath. But he wasn't taking the hint.

"Fuck this, I'm not doing it."

I stopped, mid sentence, and said "Sure, Tuck. That's you making a choice. Don't do the work, and don't get the points...but stay quiet so everyone else who *wants* to get work done, can get work done."

"Oooooh! Look at Beardman! He *almost* sounds like a *real* teacher! Isn't he *cuuuute*?"

I made a big display of rolling my neck, popping it loudly, and I put my pen down. It was about to happen. But before I could even speak, from the back corner of the room, I heard Leon thunder *"Nobody gives a fuck about your opinion, Tuck. So shut the fuck up.*"

Tucker's face reddened, and he immediately fired back "Oooooh! Coming to the defense of your boyfriend?"

Leon stood up and said "Nah. Coming to the defense of people who are tired of hearing your Shaggy lookin' bitch ass run your fuckin' mouth *and who actually want to fucking work!*"

Not to be outdone, Tucker still tried to "cool guy" it, though the scarlet creeping into his face told a different story. "This guy... this guy," he gestured at me "is complete shit."

"Because he expects you to work?" Leon countered.

Tucker gulped, trying to come up with something. "Uh. Yeah!"

"You know why you guys hate him? 'Cause he doesn't let you run around like a bunch of fucking ret*rds. Sorry for using the 'R' word, Shaw, but it's true. You fuck around in all of your classes, then bitch about how people don't give you extra time for your ADD or whatever. Guess what? School is fucking work. Come to class and fucking work. That's what we do. If you don't wanna, fine. Drop the fuck out. Go work at Mickey D's for the rest of your sad-ass life. But I want to get the fuck outta here, and you know how I do that? *I. Put. In. Fuckin.' WORK!*" The last two words were a roar that silenced the rest of the class.

Clearly out of his element, Tucker turned to me. "Oh so you're gonna write me up for a cell phone infraction, but not him for swearing?!"

"Yessir. I reckon that's about the long and short of it. Because being on your phone after I told you *four* times not to be, was wrong. Everything *he* said was right, give or take a few curse words."

"Whatever." Tucker slammed his book closed. He muttered a few things under his breath and folded his arms, and stared past me, at the dry erase board.

But Leon wasn't done.

"Go ahead and sulk like a little bitch! But guess what? You'll be in the same damn class next year. Know where *I'll* be? In college, getting better. Do you realize how many chances they fucking give you here? Y'all are fucking spoiled. See if a college teacher puts up with your shit. They won't! Or your boss? Nobody gives a *fuuuck* about what you think, *or* your feelings. You're almost out of here! The fuck you tryin' to stay another two years for?"

"If I want to, I will!"

"Yeah, sure. You're scared. Keep living at home. Keep complaining about everyone else and how they're the problem. Shaw *actually* gives a fuck about whether you pass. He's trying to help you be better...but you just wanna be weak. So keep being weak, then. But don't drag us all down with you. That's it. I'm done." Leon sat down and shook his head.

And that was it. No applause, no cheering. No nothing. But when the bell rang, I pulled Leon aside.

"Look, man. I can't give you a grade higher than an A, but you deserve it. Thanks for the assist."

He scowled at me. "I didn't do it 'cause you needed to be bailed out...I did it 'cause they need to hear truth once in awhile. I know you try, but you can't put it in the way they need to hear; the way that their parents and family *should* be saying it. I *like* that you push us when you're here. If you didn't, we'd be reading out of packets forever. Nobody fuckin' likes that shit."

I gave him the thumbs up. "You said it, man."

He shook my hand as he left, and before the door could shut, Ms. Ellston, their regular teacher, strolled in. "Anything to report, Mr. Shaw?"

"Nope. Business as usual."

May 2nd, 2014:

"Religious intolerance"

So, I was just taken to task by one of the senior girls in the transition class I've been teaching.

"Mr. Shaw? Yesterday, I felt like you were being insensitive about my religion and personal beliefs, by making jokes when I was explaining it to you."

To clarify, yesterday she told me about a "game" where

"…You start by taking a teddy bear or doll, and you, like, cut it up the middle or whatever, and scoop out the stuffing. Then you, like, take all the fingernails you've been collecting, and a cup or two of white rice, and put it into the hollow where all the stuffing was. Then, you go in the bathroom and, like, turn off all the lights. You light a black candle, and push the doll against the mirror and say 'you're it now' three times. Then you throw the doll into the tub, that you've filled with salt water, and run out of the bathroom with the candle still lit. Once you find your hiding place, you blow out the candle. Once the candle has been blown out, the doll will come looking for you. If it can't find you after three minutes, you get to live."

After sitting through that explanation patiently, I raised my hand

"Okay, couple of quick questions. First, if I only have Build A Bear stuffed animals, will that still work? From what I understand, they're imbued with some kind of love magic, so I want to make sure that I'm not crossing any energy polarities.

Second, should I be using traditional white rice? I think the only two kinds I have at home are basmati and generic brown rice. Can I use quinoa in a pinch? Because I have, like, eight bags in my pantry right now.

Third, what if I only have those Yankee Candle, jar type candles? I think the one I have is a really, really deep blue color. Is that close enough to black?

And lastly, I know that it's supposed to be dark in the bathroom…but when I go back out into the rest of the house to hide, can I keep all the other lights on? I think that it would be a lot easier to hide if I could see the doll checking around the cabinets and such with the lights on. Also, can I change hiding spots? Is there a home base?"

She got frustrated and put her headphones back on.

Guess I'm the culturally insensitive jerk now.

Chapter 5:

"The Joy Of C(r)ooking"

I was never what you would call a "bad kid," but I was a total pain in the ass, due to my constant need for attention and validation, which landed me in the principal's office more times than I'd care to admit. In 6th grade, I was trying to make friends by saying *ridiculous* things, like how my uncle worked for Nintendo "and I pretty much got whatever games I wanted for like $10 each." Eventually, a kid named Rick said "prove it." and brought in $60 and a list of games he wanted.

Shit.

On any other occasion, I would have just returned the money the following Monday, and said something like "oh he said it's only for family members" or something like that. In fact that was my plan. Unfortunately, the day he got me the $60 was the Friday before our two week holiday break, so before I could wise up, I was on a plane to Florida with $60 in my pocket. And let me tell you, friend-o: $60 buys a LOT of fireworks and ice cream in Tampa circa 1989.

When we returned, I didn't have a penny left from my adventures. First thing that Monday morning, Rick was waiting expectantly, but I had nothing. "He said there's a holdup at the company office, and it'll take a little longer." My scheming ass figured out that if I pooled my $1.25 lunch money for three months, I'd be able to pay Rick back. By week two, he was over it, and smashed me in the face when I didn't have the games. Eventually, he had his grandmother call my parents and say how "she gave him $60 of her social security and where were the games?" Not only did I have to pay my parents back, but I got grounded and a month's worth of detentions because the whole thing happened on school property.

When I was finally "asked to leave" my public high school, it was as a result of getting jumped by a bunch of spoiled rich kids (Rick among them).

One afternoon during lunch, I was hit in the back of the head while pissing in a urinal, and held down while they took turns kicking me. Ryan, the main instigator, said his goal was to "shut my fucking mouth for good" so he aimed most of his kicks at my face (and brand new braces). Stupid me turned my head to protect my mouth, which meant most of the kicks landed around my neck and ear. This later led to a massive hearing loss. When my parents pressed the (acting) principal why there was a deadbolt on the inside of the boys bathroom doors, and why five kids (four with histories of "bad" behavior) were unsupervised during that time, he shrugged and said "Mac is known for having a big mouth, and he kinda had it coming."

Ohhhh the 80s. If that kind of shit happened these days, my parents would have been able to sue the school for millions, and I probably would still be living off that sweet, sweet settlement money.

Unfortunately, that was *not* the case, and I was sent to a local Catholic school.

That was like Charlie getting the golden ticket: it was a new school, a new life, and a whole new set of goofball antics to get up to. My previous reputation quickly caught up with me, however, since bad gas travels fast in a small town. So I was back to square one.

Trying to make friends, I would bring in bulk candy from Sam's Club and sell it on the low. Then other people caught on and started doing it, eventually getting caught and souring the entire enterprise for me. How I didn't end up selling drugs is an absolute mystery--I mean, aside from being a massive scaredy cat with no poker face whatsoever.

I would often end up staying for extra help in my classes, and I quickly noticed that the teachers would write their grades in the gradebook in pencil, and only go over them in ink at the end of the semester. I watched a bunch of my teachers doing the same thing, and many of them kept their gradebooks in the back of the skinny metal drawer directly above their laps.Some of them kept the drawer locked, but most didn't. And if they *did*, you could usually get into it by mushing a small paperclip into the lock and wiggling it.

Around that time, I noticed that the drama club would meet after school, and many kids had access to the classrooms after hours "to run lines" if the gym was full. I joined up with the drama club the day I noticed *that* lovely fact, and in addition to running lines (and trying to smooch the girls in the drama club), I would also go into the grade books and change my grades. It wasn't super hard, thanks to an emphasis on the ✓, ✓+ and ✓- system most teachers used to track homework. And they would only really put zeroes in the book after tabulating weekly (or monthly) progress, so I made sure to "run my lines" before that. I was never silly about it: if I missed homework three days in a week, the most I'd re-gift myself was two checks. If a teacher had a test grade as a C-, I'd just pop a line through the minus, and boom! Instant C+.

Unfortunately, my bravado got the best of me, and one of the girls I was "practicing lines" with asked me to help change *her* grade in exchange for flashing her boobs at me.

You can probably guess where it goes from there. Word gets around, and suddenly there are two new jackasses in the drama club looking to run lines. These jerkoffs decide to start selling grades to people, and they're adding and deleting scores willy-nilly, changing F's to A's by just drawing a straight line down the right hand side. Of course, NO TEACHER IN THE HISTORY OF TIME HAS DRAWN THEIR A'S AS BLOCK LETTERS, so the teachers noticed immediately. I stopped my hustle *long* before that, and when the teachers set traps to catch the kids in the act? *Blammo!* Caught. I got away scott-free, but I learned a valuable lesson: if you're gonna do something stupid--*keep your damn mouth shut.*

Because of these shenanigans, I had a nice little magician's bag of tricks that I had collected over the years, from kids and teachers alike. Whenever I got super bored at a job, I'd create fictional heists in my head: if I wanted to cheat on a test, how would I do it? If I decided to rob the snack bar, how would I go about it? If I wanted to add emulators to all the class laptops, what would be the most efficient way? And simply by listening, I would get *so* many good ideas from kids, who would talk through their process, unknowingly giving me more tricks.

But they weren't always *good* ideas.

While working at Lil' Shawshank, conversations would inadvertently stray into inappropriate waters, and it would be my job to attempt to steer them back toward shore.

Unfortunately, it was a *good* day when I could get them to stop using Carlin's stock-standard "7 dirty words," also known as the beautiful rainbow of slurs and epithets they slung around on Snapchat, Discord, and in Call of Duty lobbies.

On one such morning, instead of swearing up a storm, Georgie and Matt took a left turn and started talking about their turns in the juvenile detention center--AKA Juvie.

"Man...I remember being, like, a master chef and shit for the guys in my house."

"Oh word? Like what?"

"Awww man. These dumb-ass hacks[7] left a whole, big-ass bag of sanitizer out in the rec room."

"Sanitizer? Like the stuff you put on your hands after you take a shit?"

"Yeah man! That shit's like *pure* alcohol. This one fat dude took the whole big ass bag, spigot and all, and hid it in his pillow."

"Awww *man!* Ok, what did you do?"

"He kept it hidden til movie night. Thursday. He'd rotate it out to different people to hold on to, so they wouldn't find it at inspection."

"Yeah?"

"Yeah, 'cause the hacks knew they fucked up, right? So they were being all polite, trying to find out where this big ass bag of sanitizer went."

"Wait...how big are we talking."

"Oh man, it was, like, twice the size of a gallon of milk!"

"So, like two gallons?"

"I don't know math, but sure. So on movie night, this guy starts doling out *big* drips into our cups. I'm talking like five or six pumps."

"Wait. you drank that shit *straight*?!?"

"Oh HELL no. We added in this Kool-Aid powder that they gave us. If you put enough powder in it, you wouldn't even taste the sanitizer…"

"Oh, *word*?"

"Yeah man. So anyway, after everyone puked a little, we got this wicked buzz going…"

"Yeah?"

"Yeah…but they…listen, shit got *bad*. Sorry, Shaw…I mean *stuff* got bad."

"Like?"

"Oh man. I almost shi…er…browned my pants."

"WHAT?"

"Yeah. There's a reason people don't drink sanitizer. That stuff'll make you poop your shorts. I had to run back to my bunk, 'cause I had bubble-guts *bad*. It kept on for the whole next day!"

"Damn."

"Yeah. I'll never do that again."

At this point, the conversation died down, and things got back to normal.

Until Georgie, not to be outdone, decided to compare recipes with Matt.

"Yo, so I never did that sanitizer thing. But I got something better."

"Oh yeah?"

"Yeah, man. You ever had Juvie LSD?"

"*WHAAAAAAAAAT!?!?!?!?!*"

At this point, Matt pulls an Aziz Ansari, and waves his skinny arms in the air, and stomps his tiny Chuck Taylors to convey his excitement.

"Yeah. Okay, dig this: you take an orange peel, right?"

"Okay, orange peel."

"Yeah, but not some, like, stupid little two-inch square of orange peel. I'm talking like a three-inch high, four-inch wide piece of orange."

"Got it."

"So you make, like a toothpaste taco."

Several seconds go by as Matt struggles to comprehend what Georgie just said. "Wait, *what?*"

"Yeah, you take the long-ass piece, then put toothpaste in the middle, then fold that shit over like a taco."

"Ohh-*kaaaay?*"

"Then, you let that cook in the sun for, like, nine days on your window sill."

"Then what?"

"Then, you *eat* it." Georgie spreads his hands out, like he just laid down a royal flush in the World Series of Poker.

"Isn't that, like, *bad* for you?"

"Oh yeah. *DEFINITELY.* But you'll trip balls for, like, 45 minutes."

"Hmmm." Max nodded his head, thoughtfully.

Now, as a guy "on the outside," I can't believe that someone would concoct something for *nine* days, for a high that *maybe* lasts for 45 minutes. And that's the *best case scenario*, considering that you stand a very real chance of becoming violently ill from consuming moldy fruit that's been tainted... er...*infused* with AquaFresh.

Eventually, I had to stop the conversation, both to keep them on track *and* to stop me from getting nauseous; it was somewhere between their recipe trading of fermented orange juice and apple juice (*"...naw man, you can't use potato skins...you need to either use carrots or banana peels!"*) and their foolproof method of growing in-cell mushrooms (*"...you wear the same socks for, like a week, then jam 'em under your bed all wet!"*).

My only hope is that we can get them into *actual* culinary programs, once they get out of here, and stop them from creating cell-inspired sock-based delights at home.

Ugh.

Speaking of lock-up, there are two big stories that stick out in my mind, both involving Lil' Shawshank. The first began years before, in Scout's classroom: in addition to teaching English, we were doing an economics enrichment program that showed the kids how to estimate taxes, build a basic budget based around a realistic monthly salary, and show them the importance of using savings accounts at credit unions vs. other banks. I loved it, mostly because budgeting wasn't really anything that was expressly taught to us in high school, and ended up being a matter of trial and error (mostly error) during my college years. One of the more outspoken kids in the class was Malik, a burly Black American kid who was bussed in from downtown. I had heard from other teachers that he had a major chip on his shoulder, but the kid was always great in my class; aside from punctuating almost every other word with *fuckin'*--and he'd apologize whenever I checked him on it.

Two years later, I ran into Malik at Lil' Shawshank, and he was *so* excited to see me. He got expelled from Scout's school for fighting in his junior year, and landed at Aspirations. He seemed to be doing well for himself, and had definitely upgraded his sneaker, clothing *and* chain game, and he seemed to garner respect from the other kids.

Two days after we were reunited, I saw him getting led out of the rec-yard by the SRO, and he was grinning the whole way. "Don't worry, Mr. S! I'll be back tomorrow!"

I never saw him again.

I had assumed that Malik got popped for possession again, since he would come to class reeking of weed daily. Not even close. I later found out that he was formally charged with pimping and pandering. *A 17-YEAR-OLD WAS CHARGED WITH PIMPING* <u>*AND*</u> *PANDERING.*

He was allegedly running a stable of girls, ages 22 to 26 via Craigslist, and was arranging everything via anonymous email account...*during school hours.* This was especially wild, considering that all students had to surrender their electronics upon walking through the gate (and after being searched). They concluded that he kept a burner smartphone in between two pairs of underwear, and would make arrangements from the single-stall boys bathroom.

He'd get an email from a john, send him a pic of the girl, text her and arrange a location. He had provided security, transportation and even paid for the girls' motel rooms. He had it all figured out...except he had neglected to pay any of the girls for two weeks, according to the SRO, and when one of them got pinched, they *all* flipped on him. They were able to triangulate the cell signal, and found the burner phone still jammed in his undies. And I kept cringing internally as I remembered telling Scout how this kid *"really* had the concept of budgeting and consumer economics figured out!"

The most intense lockup story, though, involves the aforementioned Georgie, the 6'4, 330 lb 17-year-old beast that looked like the love child of Biggie Smalls and Shaq. When he was younger, Georgie was in and out of Juvie, and was placed with a variety of families, but somehow always ended up back in a group home. For the past year, he had been living with some other family members and was rarely at school.

One morning, I noticed that one of our more emotionally-challenged students was picking at his arm and darting glances around the room. During break, I checked in with him, and he told me that he was "on a blue? Or a blue and pink?" and after taking him to the office, he told us that he cheeked[8] his meds yesterday and today, and traded it to Georgie on the bus for "something good."

Drug swapping was a *huge* no-no, and I reported it immediately. The SRO pulled Georgie into the conference room, and searched him.

He was clean.

Then I remembered that he had a metal water bottle, and it wasn't with his stuff. I said as much to the SRO, and we eventually found it wrapped in a hoodie, next to everyone's backpacks. Inside the bottle were a couple joints and a couple small baggies of pills. Not a huge haul, but definitely something he shouldn't have had at school.

Georgie was arrested, and the one visual that I'll never forget was that they needed to daisy chain the plastic restraints, because his shoulders and wrists were so wide that the traditional plastic cuffs couldn't reach.

As he was passing me on his way out to the car, he very quietly and calmly leaned in and said "I know it was you…and you *know* I'm gonna get you, right?" The SRO told him to can it, and away he went.

Now, it bears mentioning again that *I lived in the same neighborhood the school was in*, and I was constantly looking over my shoulder for the next couple months. Nothing ended up happening, and things went back to whatever passed for normal at Lil' Shawshank.

Two years later, on December 23rd, I stopped in my neighborhood Target to do some last-minute stocking stuffer shopping. As I walked through the automatic doors, I stopped to look at my hungover, scruffy-ass self in the security monitor. And then I heard the bellow.

"*YO SHAAAAAAAAWWWWW!*"

I knew that voice. Goosebumps erupted on my arms, a wave of nausea crashed over me, and it felt like ice water was shooting through my veins. I turned slowly and saw Georgie striding towards me, grinning, and the ground seemed to shake with his every step.

I'd love to tell you that I squared my shoulders and turned to face him...but I didn't. My dumb brain was so overloaded with signals, and instead of even flinching, my entire body locked up, and only my head swiveled towards him.

The only thought in my stupid lizard brain was "I should stand right here, so when I get murdered, it's all recorded on the security camera and they'll be able to tell my loved ones conclusively what happened." I shit you not. Not fight or flight; just stand right there and star in my own personal episode of MurderTV.

Georgie closed the distance in a few short steps and yelled *"IT'S BEEN A LOOOOOOOONG TIME, MOTHERFUCKER!"*

And then my feet were dangling off the ground. He had picked me up.

In a bear hug.

And he was laughing.

"OH MAN YOU SHOULD SEE YOUR FACE RIGHT NOW! DID YOU SHIT A LITTLE!? I BET YOU SHIT A LITTLE HUH!?" He set me down hard, as if sorting a stack of unruly papers.

I stared at him dumbly. "Georgie? I don't..."

"OH SHIT THAT'S RIGHT! I SAID I WAS GONNA GET YOU HUH? YEAH. SOME OTHER SHIT CAME UP." Georgie's volume control was permanently broken. It was fine--I'm half-deaf anyway.

As my body gradually began to unlock, he told me how the stuff in the bottle was actually from his aunt's boyfriend, and how he was pretty much making Georgie sell and/or carry his product around. When Georgie got pinched, he said as much to the cop, and he was removed from the house and put back into the group home. He apparently had two exemplary years, and was staying on as paid staff support, and was working towards enrolling in a trade school.

"ME GETTING SEARCHED THAT DAY WAS THE BEST THING THAT EVER COULDA HAPPENED, MAN! I FINISHED HIGH SCHOOL ONLINE AND NOW I GOT A JOB AND A GIRLFRIEND AND SHIT. SO THANKS, MAN!"

He clapped me on the back hard enough to rattle my teeth, and took off, leaving me standing there with that dumb, dazed look on my face. And then, as waves of relief washed over me, my *entire* body relaxed, and I *did* almost shit myself.

Chapter 6:

"I Wish. I. Knew Then What. I. Know. Now!"

With three years and change under my belt, I was building a pretty good stable of consistent jobs. A *huge* part of that was watching what veteran teachers did, and learning how to tweak it to work with my approach. When I found a strategy that worked well with a large group of students, I'd jot it down and stow it in my metaphorical teacher toolbox. And even though I was trying to soak up all the different teaching styles from everyone I could, some subs would just blunder through their days, weeks and months without ever looking around them.

As I mentioned before, I would watch subs blatantly pander to apathetic teachers, and staple $5 Starbucks gift cards to their daily reports. I was subbing full-time, *and* bartending/bouncing five nights a week at a couple of different joints in town just to make ends meet, so adding gift cards into my notes wasn't happening. On a "double day," I'd go into the classroom at 7 a.m., be out by 3:15 p.m., and then I'd check in at my bar job at 6:30 p.m. and leave at 3 a.m. There were many back-to-back days like that, so learning to adapt and succeed in postings was crucial.

For starters: you should *always* schmooze the secretary. All of these busters that were sucking up to the teachers and giving them incentives to request them as a substitute? Meaningless. 99% of the time, teachers request the day off, and the principal's secretary would book the assignment. Sure, the teacher might request a specific substitute, but it ultimately came down to the secretary. So I'd show up early, be extra professional, and make sure to engage them with things that were especially meaningful. It *definitely* wasn't pandering. See? I used italics to show sarcasm!

At one school, I knew the secretary volunteered at an animal rescue, so I would occasionally ask what events were upcoming, and promote them on Facebook. Another loved college sports, and as an ISU alum, I'd look up stats and talking points, so it seemed like I loved sports too.

When in doubt, I would *always* defer to the secretary, and even pick up odd classes and periods that needed extra coverage. And I'd almost always get results in the classes I covered. One secretary said "well, I've been giving you all of the challenging classes, because you seem to be the only substitute that can get any work out of 'em!"

It was all a con: say a teacher assigned three pieces of work that each student was responsible for completing. I'd look at the day's agenda and tack on extra work without telling the kids. For example, if the teacher assigned three pages of work, I'd say something like
"Alright everybody, look. Your teacher wants me to assign five..."
I'd squint at the plan "FIVE pages of work. Holy crap, that's a lot."
The kids would groan.

"I *know*! Ok, tell you what: if you can all knock out *three* pages worth of work, I'll tell her that you all were working *so* incredibly hard, that three was all you could possibly do. How does that sound?"

Cheers all around.

One thing I wish I learned sooner? Bring your lunch in a cooler, and don't bring things that need to be heated up. All too often, teachers are pressed for every last second in a school day, so you'll see grown adults literally sprinting for the bathroom, because little Billy had to stay after class and ask 8 minutes worth of questions. Finding your way to the staff lounge was another time suck, as was waiting for a microwave. Plus, I can't tell you how often grown-ass adults would "accidentally" eat my lunch from the staff fridge. So yeah, if you're gonna sub, invest in a nice hard-sided cooler and stow it under your desk.

Want to be beloved by all? The next time you're at the grocery store, grab a case of cheap fruit snacks and granola bars, and keep a handful of each in your work bag. You wouldn't believe how many kids skip breakfast because they're getting their siblings ready for school. Just having a healthy-ish burst of sugar shaped like animated characters is almost enough to win anyone over.

Lastly? Talk to the students like they're people. Be direct and honest, and don't pander. If they ask you a direct question, and you have the ability to answer it directly, do so. Don't try to lob them a slow-pitch softball answer if they ask a fastball question. Pay attention to their reaction to your answer, and ask follow-up questions. Or better yet, encourage *them* to ask clarifying questions if your answer was too complex. Building an environment where kids are comfortable asking for clarification is huge, because you're strengthening their ability to problem-solve and troubleshoot independently.

December 11th, 2015:

"Never ask my opinion"

I just witnessed the parent of a high school student come in and scream at the secretary for 10 minutes.

I walked into the office in time to hear her shriek "WHAT THE FUCK ARE YOU PEOPLE DOING HERE? I'm trying to keep this little shit on lockdown and you people? YOU PEOPLE let him get away with murder!"

The exchange went on for a little while, and the secretary apologized profusely, all while the mother kept screeching and waving a tiny packet in her face.

"WHAT IF IT WAS METH? OR HEROIN! WHAT WOULD YOU HAVE DONE THEN?"

She was starting to make my head hurt, so I approached to learn more...and hopefully shut her the fuck down. Plus, I recognized her son as one of my students from a couple months back.

Turns out, the kid used his debit card to order his girlfriend a cubic zirconia ring from QVC like website and had it shipped to the school. He somehow had it labeled as college material, so it would be lumped in with all the other college packets that are currently being delivered by the truckload.

Smart.

After I got the gist, she whirled on me. "And what do YOU think about all this?!"

"I think you have an incredibly clever son who's clearly embarrassed and upset by your reaction. Judging by the x's drawn on his hands, drugs will probably be the LAST thing he's buying via mail. And if he's going to continue to shop online using your credit card, he should probably invest in a P.O. box."

The kid smiled weakly as his mother exploded.

"Oh yeah? OH YEAH? THANKS FOR THAT TIP! AND WHEN HE HACKED THE COMPUTER SYSTEM LAST YEAR THE REASON HE WAS EXPELLED WOULD YOU HAVE RECOMMENDED THAT HE GET A BETTER COMPUTER!?"

"No, because you don't necessarily need a better computer to write better code. And if I recall correctly, he changed one grade, from a B- to an A-. Granted, it was wrong and he's dealing with the consequences, but he's also on track to graduate a YEAR early. And in every class of mine that he's been in, he's fantastic: finishes every assessment early, contributes relevant discussion to class and is self motivated. What I would RECOMMEND is looking into scholarship possibilities to RIT or MIT."

"AM I TAKING FUCKING CRAZY PILLS? I CAN'T DO THIS SHIT ANYMORE! FUCK IT!" she stormed out the double doors in a whirlwind of snot, tears and howls.

The kid stared at me, incredulous.

"Don't look at me, dude. She's YOUR mom."

Chapter 7:

"Help Me I Am In (h)ELL"

Throughout my various gigs, both long- and short-term, I encountered teenagers from all socioeconomic strata, and from cultures all over the world. The district I had primarily settled into was a genuinely diverse grouping of students from all over the county, where some students lived in 1.5 million dollar houses...and others lived out of their cars.

I got a ping on my SubFinder app one morning with a full-day listing for an ENG/ELL posting, and since teaching English tended to be my strength, I immediately accepted the assignment.

When I accepted the gig, the purely 'Merican side of me didn't stop to realize that in addition to immigrant students, we take in thousands of refugees every day...and many of those refugees have children who don't speak a word of English.

As a result, many schools have had to add ELL versions of their classes, as well as Sheltered English Immersion courses for brand-new learners that have never experienced the English language before.

We, as Americans, are so warm inside our cultural bubble, that we expect that just because *we* want to be here, every other immigrant and refugee wants to be here, too. After all, why else would you leave your war-torn country, if not to live in our gold-paved Land of Opportunity? I never stopped to think that many of the families are here out of necessity, and self-preservation... not because they *really* wanted to be here.

Around the second year, I worked in a couple of such classrooms in our district, and the teachers liked having me there...mainly because I don't startle easily. The classes tended to be a little louder, a little more aggressive than other traditional classes, and as a result, it was often hard to find substitutes for them.

I have overheard other substitutes *and even other teachers* talking down about the EL students. "They're rude" is the flat description I most often heard. One time, I overheard an academic coach say "her scars creep me out, and the way she touches things with that nub is *gross*." The student she was referring to? A 16-year-old refugee who had scars up the side of her face and neck, and was missing her left hand.

"Have you ever talked with her?" I interrupted the coach.

"*Excuse* me?"

"The girl you're talking about. Addie. Do you know why she's missing her hand?"

The two coaches backpedaled, realizing I overheard them. "Oh. No. Not at all. And just so you're aware: we were, uh, talking about a new scary movie trailer..."

"Oh, got it. Which trailer? I *love* scary movies!"

The woman paled. "Uh...I forgot the name." They hastily began to pack up their lunch.

"...Because if you *ever* end up talking about Addie--you know--in the future? You ought to remember that she survived an explosive blast, and her family can't afford to get her a replacement limb yet. So she's kicking ass with the use of only one hand. And the new movie you were talking about?" The girls stared at me, cow-eyed. "You were discussing it loud enough that my half-deaf ass could hear you AND *I* knew who you were talking about. Y'know, *just so you're aware*.

The biggest challenge with teaching classes like this, is that 90% of the kids are *way* smarter than they let on. As a result, they can smile and shrug, and say "no understand English," and teachers will fall all over themselves to break down what they already totally understand. Sure, there most definitely *are* kids that don't get it, but they're pretty easy to spot. Mainly because they look, well, *confused*...and aren't smirking.

But by far the biggest problem I've found with their ethnocentrism is that for many of them, shaking their patriarchal and/or fundamentalist religious roots simply isn't on the agenda. Sure, for political/survival reasons, they're relocated to America, but damned if they're going to become Americanized while they're here! Hey, I'm all for sticking close to your roots, but once you're in the American school system, you need to respect *our* cultural expectations, as well as the varied cultures and customs of other students in the class.

Namely, equality.

In one of my classes, Alvin, a chubby Iraqi student, openly catcalled and heckled a girl named Shanna, in the class while she attempted to give a speech on her research project. After shushing him three times, I finally had her pause, and addressed him in front of the whole class.

"Why can't you show Shanna the same respect she showed you, and keep quiet while she's presenting?"

He scoffed. "Respect? *A girl?* No. Not today. Not any day." He said something in Arabic, and the other male students around him tittered. Shanna, clearly flustered, threw down her cue cards.

I turned back toward Alvin. "So if she was a male, you'd be quiet? You're being rude just because she's a woman?"

"Girl," he corrected me. "She's *just* a girl. And a messy girl to begin with. She deserves no quiet."

"Really? So you think it's ok to judge people on their gender, or for something they can't change?"

He shrugged, indifferent. "She messy, too."

"So it's ok to demean someone because they're messy? You're telling me, if I made a rule that all students with B.O. and sloppy facial hair got an automatic F, that would be fair?" The class starts to giggle.

Alvin scowled at me. "What is B.O.?!"

"B.O. is body odor. Armpit stink." I mimed smelling my pits. "The whole 'not showering for a week' during the summer months isn't doing anyone any favors. Ladies? Am I right?"

The girls sitting on either side of him nodded, and covered their faces with their hands. He reddened.

He spat something else in Arabic at me.

"Alvin, you know that I don't understand what you're saying. But from your body language, I'm thinking that you understand me *perfectly*. So, for the rest of the day, every negative comment you levy at Shanna, or any of the other girls, chips a letter off your project grade. And don't even think of saying something in Arabic, 'cause I'll have Rania over there translate for me."

"BUT WHAT IF I SAY SOMETHING IN MY LANGUAGE THAT'S GOOD, AND SHE LIES AND SAYS I SAID SOMETHING BAD!?!"

"Well, Alvin, I guess you have to hope that she's doing the right thing...y'know, respecting you and all. Or, here's a novel thought: maybe don't say anything in Arabic, which could be misunderstood as bad. Or! Even better yet? *Don't say anything at all.*"

The girls hooted as Alvin slammed his book on the desk.

He wouldn't make eye contact with me, and instead rapped his knuckles on the book, agitated.

"Oh, and one last thing, Alvin: if you can't keep the beat, you're not allowed to drum. Knock it off."

He jammed his hands in his pockets and glared at me.

I looked back at Shanna. She was beaming.

"So sorry for the interruption, Shanna. Please continue?"

She did continue, and she knocked it out of the park. I ended up giving her an A-, because even though her speech was flawless, she forgot to attach her sources.

Hell, I'm nice...but I'm not *that* nice!

April 21st, 2015:

"Bahgawd!"

So I had this fantastic moment yesterday in the "Sheltered English Immersion" program, which consists mainly of refugees and children in great need of an education...who have never spoken English before.

The classroom is the very definition of a melting pot.

Recently, we got a student (let's call him Tim) who is from a Micronesian island, and speaks a language that's a pidgin language of ANOTHER pidgin language. So there's quite literally no interpreter we could use.

In short, traditional communication is next to impossible, and we can't really give him a basis for comparison...so it's all new to him.

Another student (let's call him Jeff) had been caught sneaking his cell phone four times, so I pointed at him, pointed at the phone, frowned and did the universal "thumb drawn across the neck" to nonverbally call him out without bothering the rest of the class. Jeff laughed, powered off his phone and put it in his bag. Easy.

From behind me, I hear Tim mumble "tumstone...tumstone piledriver."

I turned around. "What?"

Tim mimicked the "thumb across neck" thing, smiled hugely, and said "Unnr taker. Tumstone. Lass ride!"

I was stunned. I mimicked pulling a glove on, and the kid clapped and said "CHOKE SLAM!"

The entire class was dialed into Tim, and his excitement was catching.

I mimicked the Triple H entrance and he giggle screamed "THE GAAAAAAME!"

For the rest of the class, the boys surrounding Tim chattered excitedly, throwing out names and moves, and pulled up classic matches on their phones and laptops.

By lunchtime, Tim (who previously ate his lunch in the hallway, alone) had a new squad, and even though they couldn't necessarily speak each other's language, they were able to connect over something as ridiculous as 90s white trash, American professional wrestling. Wild.

Chapter 8:

"My Wholly Unsurprising Fall From Grace"

Right around my long-term stint in the EL classroom, I was feeling incredible. It actually reminded me of when I would do stand-up sets, first at open mics and later as a "middler"; each day would begin with an introduction, then I'd need to maintain their attention for the rest of the class time. It was a challenge that never ceased to be exhilarating.

Whenever I'd start a class, I'd open with something like this:

"GOOOOOOD MORNING (name of school)!! I'm not going to start with that 'let's try that again/I can't hear you' crap, because you're not six. Show of hands, who has had me before? Excellent. What can you tell your fellow students about me?" This was a softball, because it was usually something positive: "you're funny," "you're half-deaf," etc. and by having their peers talk me up, it would usually bring the rest of the class around to being on my team.

"I have but two commandments: no cell phones and no talking while I'm talking. The cell phones are a huge thing, because the last time I was here, I let the class use their phones whenever they wanted...and pictures of me ended up on the Internet." At this point, I had everyone's undivided attention, and a couple would be leaning forward in their seats.

"It's true. I ended up on their Snapchats, Facebook and Insta's with the hashtag Hottest Sub Ever! Do you know how it feels to delete three thousand DMs without reading them? It's rough! And I'm not an object, and refuse to be treated like one!" This never failed to get a solid laugh, and if that joke landed, I usually had them for the day.

"The second commandment is 'no talking when I'm talking.' It's not that old man thing of 'you'll respect me when I'm speaking;' no, it's this." I'd point at my hearing aid. *"I know, I know. When you came in, you were like 'is that the world's fattest Secret Service agent?' No. It's my hearing aid. And when I'm talking and someone starts talking at the same time, the microphone fights for signal, and it sounds awful, like silverware in a garbage disposal...or Nickelback."* (I'd swap out whichever pop musician was getting dragged at the moment). This was the second part of the two-hit joke--if it landed, I was safe.

To finish it out, I'd usually say *"Now...what questions can I answer?"* This is a sneaky teacher trick that I swear by, because if you say "do you have any questions?" kids will all look at each other like "if you shut up, we might get out of here early!" But by phrasing it as "what questions can I answer?" normalizes the act of asking for clarification.

"What questions can I answer?" is a trap, of course. During the previous bit about "no talking while I'm talking," I would be unbuttoning my right shirt cuff and slowly rolling up my sleeve, to reveal my tattoos. I would finish cuffing my left sleeve as I asked "what questions can I answer?" knowing full well that

half the class would have a tattoo-related question, which was a perfect time to roll into *"well, we have a lot of work to finish today, but I promise you this: if you can all show me that you completed the work before the end of the period, we'll spend the last ten minutes doing a Q&A. Sound good?!"* This was always met with a resounding "YES!"

Of course, there would be 20 hands up at the end of class waiting to ask questions, and I'd be sure to stretch each answer into 4-5 minutes, ensuring that I couldn't answer all the questions *this* time. As the bell rung, I'd call out *"I'll be sure to get to anyone I missed today,* next *time I'm here!"* This all but ensured that the kids would give a stellar report to the teacher, and the teacher would see that all of the day's work was completed. Kids loved me, teachers never complained about my teaching style, and I felt like I was invincible.

This is how I managed to have repeat customers consistently. Problem was, even though I'd have 85% of classes and teachers singing my praises, I'd have the other 15% grumbling about my style. "He's not professional enough," "he has challenges speaking to other staff" and "he doesn't consistently use appropriate classroom language" were some of the common complaints, and on paper, it looked daunting. In my seven-ish years with that particular district, I got two "write-ups" which equated to being blacklisted from two schools. Of course, I didn't ever find that out until I went in to request a copy of my file when I was about to change districts....but more on that later.

The biggest problem with these write-ups (aside from them sitting in my file without anyone mentioning them), was that the language was incredibly vague and I wasn't able to get clarification on any except the "doesn't consistently use classroom appropriate language" complaint. If you were to base my performance solely on those documents, it *sounds* like I would stroll into the room and yell "ALRIGHT YOU LITTLE MOTHERFUCKERS, LET'S GET THIS SHIT SHOW ON THE

FUCKIN' ROAD" as I put out my Lucky Strike on a kid's forehead.

Come to find out, it was the "hashtag hottest sub ever" line that the kids were laughing about the day after I covered the class. And the kicker? It wasn't even a complaint from the teacher I covered for...but another teacher eavesdropping on kids talking at lunch. *"He's in the class telling kids how hot he is, and how is* that *appropriate when you're talking to 16- and 17-year olds?"* She mentioned that to the assistant principal, who immediately wrote up a complaint. After all, they take these things "very seriously"...just, y'know, not seriously enough to pull me aside and actually *talk* to me about it.

The one complaint that I *did* deserve came a year later when I was covering an English as a second language class for two solid weeks. As I mentioned before, ELL (or "sheltered English") classes are incredibly challenging because many of the kids tend to be refugees, asylum-seekers and/or "placed" in the program.This means that they're often viewed as outsiders by other students, and tend to "pod up" with people who speak their own language. Add to that, the classrooms are usually overfilled, with 15-20 extra students in each class, many without any interpreter support. The last nail in the coffin is that students tend to be placed in these classes regardless of ability, so you'll have a student that's a fluent reader/speaker of Urdu, but they're put alongside other students that are just learning a basic command of their native language, which often results in frustration and boredom...the two worst ingredients you can have in a volatile environment.

By the fourth day, I was getting to know the kids and telling them about myself and becoming comfortable with the classroom. High fives and fruit snacks were our primary currency, and the kids were especially chatty and jokey. In previous classrooms, if tensions were rising, I would usually try to dissolve it with humor. After a couple years dealing with aggressive hecklers in comedy audiences, I had gotten better at riffing off a student's diss. The problem was I subbed the majority of my days at Lil' Shawshank, so I was used to my students having thicker skin.

In this particular instance, I had Miles, an 18-year-old Arabic student that was *this* close to being exited from the EL program, which would put him into traditional mainstream classes instead of the EL class. In the short time I worked with him, it was evident that he was significantly higher in terms of comprehension, language acquisition and retention. During lessons, he would power through his assignments and spend the rest of the class lobbing insults at me and his fellow students. By day four, he realized that I wasn't going to throw him out of the class, so he would entertain his friends by getting jabs in on me, the majority of which were in his native language. This evoked peals of laughter from his friends.

"Oh what did I miss now," I asked, exasperated. The group snickered and Miles said "I just...I just told them how much I like your shirt." More howls of laughter from his table. The other 20-something students just sat there, eyes big, waiting for the inevitable detention or reprimand.

When the laughter died off, I rolled my eyes and continued the lesson. Miles raised his hand.

"Mista Shaw? You know that you look like the fat guy that does the song from Shrek right?" His table exploded with laughter, banging on the desk and hooting.

Without missing a beat, I said "...and you remind me of Shock G, Miles! Let's tour and make some of that D-list celebrity money!" I mimed making it rain, and the class laughed.

It's important to note: this kid was a dead ringer for Shock G with his Buddy Holly glasses, bushy eyebrows and bulging eyes, but none of the kids had the slightest idea who that was. At lunchtime, apparently a couple kids looked him up, and the table spent the rest of the day singing the hook to "The Humpty Dance" at him nonstop.

I thought it was done after lunch, since Miles stopped throwing barbs at me. When he got home, he told his parents that his loud white teacher compared him to a black guy, and Miles, who *wasn't* black, took it very personally. His parents called the school the following morning and demanded that I be removed. The acting principal at the time, a harried woman who looked far older than her years and gave off an air of continual exhaustion, called me in before Friday's class and asked for clarification. So I told her that I try to dissolve tension in the classroom with humor, and none of what I said was mean or mean-spirited. I explained the situation, and exactly what I said to the student, as clearly and directly as possible. "I let him roast me throughout the week," I said "and I thought the touring joke would have won him over, since we both look like celebrities."

"*Well it didn't!*" she screeched. "His parents complained and demanded that you be removed from this class. I'm going to report this to the district, and will likely ask you not to come back to this location." I was shook. "I've been in classrooms where teachers would use profanities in their daily lessons *and* cuss out students, and I've done none of those things."

She pursed her lips together "why would you *ever* think that 'roasting' a student would be appropriate?"

"You think *that* was a roast?" I asked her, genuinely curious. "The intention wasn't to hurt the kid...or even mock him. It was to riff off his insult."

She rolled her eyes and stood up. "The district will be in touch."

I felt cold inside; not only did I shoot myself in the foot in terms of a consistent job that was less than a mile from my house, but I unintentionally hurt a student. It was at this point that I realized that something had to change in my approach. I wouldn't necessarily stomp the brakes on my approach to classroom management, but I would also try to be more open-minded about what could and could not be perceived as offensive or hurtful to students. After all, regardless of how mature these kids seem to act, it's important to remember that we might be the only adult in their life that *doesn't* talk down to them. And even though they sling around sarcasm like it's a second language, having a teacher be sarcastic to them can feel especially one-sided.

So I deserved it. It sucked, but a wiser man than myself once said it best: *"the dildo of consequences rarely arrives lubed."*

Failure can provide a valuable lesson, provided that you actually *learn* from it. So I stood back up, dusted myself off, and kept moving forward.

Chapter 9:

"Trying My Hardest To Be The Shepherd..."

Ever since I was just a little tater tot, I was taught to question authority.

The 80s were a turbulent time, and kidnappings were all the rage...at least, that's what the nightly news would have you believe. As a result, I was taught to loudly ask "WHO ARE YOU!?" to strangers if they attempted to spirit me away in a car. Hell, my mother even went as far as letting me create my own secret phrase[9], so I'd know that the person picking me up was *really* who they said they were. Middle school taught me to seek more answers if I was looking for something more; to dig deeper if something really piqued my interest. That Indiana Jones-ian thirst for knowledge followed me into college, where I was the annoying kid looking for further clarification as to *why* something was the way it was. My journalism professor taught me the old adage that I still live by today: *"if your mother tells you that she loves you, you should always get a second opinion."*

In short: don't always believe your sources, and dig, dig, dig.

Growing up, whenever I was in the confines of the classroom, if a teacher set out rules, they were usually expected to be followed to the letter.

Did *I* follow them to the letter? Rarely. But that didn't change the fact that I knew what disobeying meant. I mean, I knew what would happen *if I got caught*. The funny thing was I never held my punishment against my teachers. I may have been an annoying prick, prone to all sorts of shenanigans, but when I got caught, I accepted my punishment. After all, it's not like I wasn't bound by the same list of expectations as everyone else. If I didn't get caught, it was a rush. And if I did? Well, good game; I'd concede and take my lumps.

Because of my childhood, I'm a bit more versed in the ways of jackassery than some of the other teachers I work with, and as I said before: if my students get one over on me, they're rewarded...and I get another entry in my book of tricks.

Despite my overly gruff demeanor, I'm a *big* believer in second chances...especially with the "problem" kids I'm constantly saddled with. 9 times out of 10, they're just looking for attention; and negative reinforcement is the quickest way to get that attention.

I'm not going to be an armchair parent at all, but I *can* speak about the students I've worked with in the past. Sure, they can be a handful, but they still deserve the same attention, love, and support we have to give...and that support shouldn't end in the classroom.

Instead, I'm seeing dull-eyed students that talk about *"what fucking bitches/assholes"* their parents are. Not once or twice, but every. Damn. Day. You won't believe me when I tell you, but 50% or more of my kids flat-out *tell* me how ineffectual or absent their parents are, with concrete examples. I'm not talking the standard *"nobody gets me/people are dogshit/I hate my life/*

everything is pointless" ennui that plagues teenagers; I'm talking rock-solid, depressing tales of how nobody at home tells them that they love them.

Or hugs them.

Or notices that they got all A's. Or all B's. Or are passing for the first time in their life.

Or never come to watch them play sports.

Or doesn't show up for their presentations, recitals or exhibitions.[10]

Or takes the time to actually *talk* to them.

Or spends time listening to *their* kid's problems without piling on their own.

So when I'm a little easier on my kids, it's with good reason. I'm not going to coddle them or be the teacher that just shrugs and says "LOL I dunno" when they fuck up; I'm the one that painstakingly explains *why* I'm so pissed. By using "I feel..." statements and conditional phrasing (e.g. "when you knock over my chair, it makes me feel frustrated"), I try to reinforce the "why" behind my response. And when they act out, I remind them that this is a *conscious decision* that they're making, and to think about the outcome, both long- and short-term.

But.

There's a fine, fine line between understanding and weakness: if you're that parent that keeps holding "*or else!*" over their head, they'll end up with the *wrong* idea of questioning authority. Because of that, at <u>least</u> once a day, I have a student that says "*or what?*" to me.

There are few things in my personal little *Shaw*verse that grind my gears quite as thoroughly as those two words.

106

"Or what?"

In *my* classroom, "or what" is worse than "fuck you." To me, after I ask three or four times for someone to be compliant, when the response is *"or what?"* it's tantamount to saying *"you aren't gonna do shit, motherfucker"* At that point, you just shot the hostage negotiator, and there's **absolutely no going back.**

Not only that, but the chances are pretty high that they said that in a room full of their peers. If I *don't* do anything, word will spread like wildfire, and by lunchtime, I'll be the guy that lets everything slide. By the *next* day, I'll be lucky if I can get the students to take out their books.

That's why *"or what?"* opens the floodgates for me; until then, I've let everything else slide. Now I'm backed into a corner, and something *has* to happen.

This is when I dig out my *special* detentions.

Many schools, like many fast food companies, have a "secret menu" of punishments to choose from; not just the standard "detention or suspension" choices...and they're downright *creative*:

> Some schools have tiered detentions, where you can assign someone 3:45-4:45 detention, instead of the standard "2:45 to 3:45," which means that they'll actually be getting TWO detentions instead of one, since they're forced to stay at school an extra hour, and wait for *their* detention time to start.

> I've worked for schools that have "Outside Saturday School" where kids come in at 7 a.m. on a Saturday, and complete 5 hours of manual labor, including planting flower beds, picking up trash from the school grounds, transferring one massive pile of dirt 10 feet to the right (and back again, the

following week).

Academic Recidivist ISS which, in addition to "regular" in school suspension, forces students to take an extra weekend "self-management" class, consisting of six (!) essays, an apology letter, and completion of several "stress tests" (all of which are checked and graded), as well as a signed declaration saying that the student will be expelled if this (*insert action here*) occurs again.

A personal favorite of mine is "Career shadowing," which is just a fancy way of saying that you'll be shadowing the janitor/maintenance specialist for 1 to 3 days after school, during which you'll be cleaning toilets, scrubbing graffiti off walls, mucking drains, scrubbing out dumpsters, emptying trash cans and mopping floors. This punishment is perfect for kids who like to vandalize school property.

The major point here is, since they're nearly (or in some cases, *are already*) adults, I will treat them as such. Respect goes both ways, and if I'm going to take the time to patiently explain why I'm asking you *not* to do something reasonable, I expect that you have enough respect to follow suit.

My classroom is your job: follow directions, pay attention, do solid work and you'll get rewarded. If you refuse? Well, maybe this "job" just wasn't the right fit for you. And every minute that I'm wasting appeasing your need for attention is a minute that I could be spending on students who actually *want* to be here and are listening, working and actively participating.[11]

High school is designed to prepare our teenagers for the real world...it's high time to start treating them like the adults they are, not the Teflon children they *pretend* to be.

But as parents? Start hugging your kids. Ask them how their

day was *and mean it.* Take an **active** interest in their lives, and hopefully you can give them the attention they need, before they come looking for negative reinforcement from *me.*

And for *fuck's sake* can we please cut out the "bulldozer parenting?" Bulldozer parents march straight into school to forcibly remove every obstacle in their child's way. I can't tell you how many useless meetings I've had to sit through where parents try to tell me that their kid "shouldn't have to do homework" and how I should allocate time into class to allow them to complete their homework at school. At that point, I will usually write HOMEWORK on a sheet of paper, and ask them what the first four letters spell.

Honest to God, for everyone who complains about how kids are soft today, look at the over-coddling parents. And stop thinking that we should reward mediocrity. Just because your darling child was able to vomit a page worth of words into a Google Doc doesn't mean they should get an A. In fact, for every misspelled word on digital assignments they submit to me, I take a minimum of 10 points off. *You're writing on a device that* literally *checks your spelling for you!* Take responsibility for your own damn work!

And yet, year after year, I have long meetings where a parent plaintively begs that their kids' work be resubmitted for an A, despite them not showing growth during their revisions. It's gotten to the point, where I'll stop a contentious meeting and ask the parent say "look, we can keep going around and around, but you're not telling me what you *really* want out of this meeting. So, since our shared time is valuable, can you tell me exactly what you're hoping to get today?"

And then I'll spend the next ten minutes eviscerating their request, and explaining why they *won't* get it.

Meanwhile, other parents will come into these meetings asking "how can my child pass this year?" And honestly, if they come in early enough, I'll set up a plan with them where we can tag-team support for their kiddo, and they'll actually have to *try* to fail my class. They won't pass with an A, but they'll get the grade they deserve.

This small action of showing them (and their parents) that positive progress *is* attainable is why I do what I do. Failing something is how we learn, as humans, how to succeed--it's called "failing forward" and I hope some parents eventually come around to seeing it.

All of my kids know: I don't *give* grades--hard work, dedication and a willingness to get extra help will always be rewarded in my room. If I see a kid staying after, asking questions, and pushing a little harder, you bet your ass that their 76 might magically turn into an 81 overnight. My job is to track progress, and if I can demonstrate your kid is showing growth through nontraditional evaluation (verbal answers, in-depth artwork, group presentations, etc.), by God they will be rewarded for it. And any teacher worth their salt should be doing the same thing.

Let's build better, more resilient people; people who will problem-solve, and look at challenges from a solution-based perspective. Voicing your problems without offering realistic solutions is just whining, and the world has more than enough fucking whiners.

June 8th, 2018:

"Shoelace Shakubuku"

In the midst of all of this morning's weirdness, I had an amazing exchange with a student named Max. Throughout this year, Max has struggled with depression and has a home life that's challenging to say the least.

He's currently working, has been accepted to college and is looking forward to getting out of his hometown. He's saving up all of his money so that he can move out, and experience life in a new part of the country. I believe in him wholeheartedly: he's thoughtful, kind and polite to a fault, and I'm excited to see what he does when he's not held down by a negative environment.

Almost every morning this year, he comes in bummed out, either overtired from work last night, or with leftover stress from home.

This morning was completely different: he strode in beaming, with two boxes of doughnuts held on high, like he was announcing the next Lion King.

I was floored.

He set the boxes down with a flourish, and said "My life changed last night."

I tried to keep a poker face. "Go on."

"Ok, so I've been grappling with this shit all year. You know. And last night I was at my lowest point. Seriously. So I kinda fell down a rabbit hole on YouTube, and it just got steadily worse. So around 3 a.m., I just said 'fuck this!' and I pulled on a hoodie, my favorite pair of sneakers, grabbed my keys and went out into my neighborhood. After walking around for an hour, I had an idea. I realized that if I was going to do something huge, I'd need to make a sacrifice."

My eyes widened. I didn't like where this was going.

"...So I took off my sneakers, balled up my socks, mushed them down into the shoes. I tied the laces together and threw 'em up and over the telephone lines that ran along the park near my house. My favorite shoes. That was my sacrifice."

I exhaled slowly.

"I realized that that was the first time I had felt wet grass on my bare feet in 10 years. It was nice just to be alone and feel something. Like that moment was mine and mine alone."

"Oh yeah?"

"Well, except for the tweeker doing jumping jacks on the other side of the park."

I stifled a laugh. "Go on."

"I got to thinking: if I'm the protagonist of my own story, then there HAS to be an antagonist. There just HAS TO BE. Same for if I was the antagonist of my life...I'd be put in place by a protagonist. Because that's how it goes in EVERY story."

"Pretty much, yeah."

"So I figured: there's no time like right now. It's 3:30 a.m., nobody's around. I wasn't gonna get another chance like this. So I called out my enemy."

"Come again?"

"I screamed at the sky. WHAT THE FUCK ARE YOU WAITING FOR!? COME FUCKING GET ME! I'M FUCKING READY! COME FUCKING GET IT! And I waited."

I leaned in, eyes as wide as saucers. "What happened?"

"Nothing," he exhaled deeply. "Absolutely nothing."

"Wait...so what was your revelation?"

"That there is no big enemy...no big bad guy. There just is this." He fanned his hands out in front of him, gesturing at the room.

"Wait, so the big anti hero was...jazz hands?"

He snickered. "NO! The whole thing was that there WAS no enemy. It was just me and a mostly empty park. But that was ok. Because I had the feeling of the wind at night...the wet grass squishing between my toes. The coldness of each breath. It was beautiful."

"You know why that is, right?"

"Huh?"

"Why there was no big hero or anti hero out to get you?"

He shrugged. "I didn't get that far."

"You're not the hero of your story, and you're definitely not the villain."

"Then what the fuck am I!?"

I smirked at him. "You're the writer."

His jaw dropped, and I waved him out of the room.

The next morning, he rushed in breathless "If I'm the writer, then I can write a story where I actually do something! If I create positivity in my world, then I'll feel all that positivity reflected back at me."

"That's the idea, yeah. Doesn't always work out that way, though."

"Oh, like people that just take the positivity you give 'em and don't reflect it? What do you do then?"

"Then you give 'em more. You drown 'em in it. Think of it this way: If you give someone with no money 50 bucks, they'll use it to buy something from someone, then that person will have 50 bucks. But if the person has negative 120 bucks in their account, even if you give 'em 50 bucks, they're still at negative 70 bucks. So you might need to give them a little bit more."

"Oh. That makes sense, I guess."

"So you still want to give positivity to the masses?"

He smirked, "You never know until you try, right?"

"Right. And don't forget to lift yourself up, too. Take care of yourself as well! Treat yourself."

"Treat yourself?"

I nodded back at him. "Treat yourself."

"...And any chance that I can get that 50 bucks you mentioned?"

"No."

Chapter 10:

"This Is Only A Test"

If there is one thing I loathe that stands out head-and-shoulders above the multitude of things that gnaw at me each day, it's *learned helplessness.*

I only subbed in high schools, and the young ladies and gentlemen that filter through my classrooms are on the very cusp of being adults (and for some "Super Seniors"[12]...*they're already there*). These young people will soon make significant life choices once they cross into the magical numeric realm of 18.

I'm making the assumption that you, dear reader, are over 21. Maybe you've already bested the perils of college, with Tuesday parties that end at 4 a.m. and first-light Wednesday classes that begin at 7:10. You've "puked and rallied," you've started the desperate, frantic search of finding a post-school (or during-school) job. You've sweated and agonized over interviews, gone on awkward dates. You've dashed away all of your weekend free time with friends and family (or Netflix), when you probably should have done some laundry and cleaned your apartment like you promised yourself you would.

Let's face it: once you hit 21, every passing year seems to speed by faster than the last.

Now, take that limited grasp of time and realize the precarious situation that we as teachers are in: we have 4 years (barely 3 if you take winter, spring and summer vacations into account) to mold our students into human adults capable of surviving out in the big, bad world.

The major problem is that our baby-faced Freshmen are coming to us as empty, test-taking husks. Sure, they can bubble in Scantrons, puzzle out the "best" answer, and bullshit their way through an essay by repeating the same premise in different ways...but they can't tell you *why* they came to that conclusion.

What's worse is the new cavalcade of "I don't know" students. This goes beyond Chris Rock's famous "it's cool to be dumb" hypothesis and plunges headlong into Twilight Zone territory.

For example, John, a new student in one of my classes, raised his hand no less than 12 times during a "silent project" that I had designed for the students, where they would read information, then use the provided prompt to express their own thoughts on the paragraph.

"Mr. Shaw," John pointed at the question sheet. "I don't understand this."

"Which part?"

"This. #2. It says 'How do Starla's problems compare to mine?' Who's Starla?"

"Did you read the passage?"

"No. The question doesn't make sense. Who's Starla?"

I took a deep breath. "Starla is the girl that the paragraph is about. Read the paragraph before you try to answer the questions."

"Oh, like for all of them?"

"Yes. What do the directions say?"

"Read the passage below and answer the questions on the following page in your own words."

"Ok."

Ten minutes later, John raises his hand again. "So I'm supposed to re-word the questions in my own words?"

"No, John. You're supposed to *answer* the questions in your own words."

"Ohhh...ok."

I spent the next 10 minutes walking around the room, checking everyone's work. Almost everyone "got" it, but half the class had answered the questions oddly. When I came around to John again, I peeked at his work.

3.) Do any of Starla's family members mirror your own?

I don't remember anything about a mirror in the story. Starla has family members and so do I.

He was on question #5, and only rehashed the same information in the question for every answer. I pulled him aside, quietly. "John, what did you take away from the passage?"

"What?"

"The passage, before the question--what was the main idea?"

"I dunno."

"Did you forget? Are the words not making sense?" As a kid with ADHD and dyslexic tendencies, I was looking for the telltale processing challenges with John.

"No. But I skimmed it and tried to answer the questions."

"Ok. I want you to read, *not skim*, the whole thing, ok? *Then* answer the questions. The article is barely a page long."

"Ok."

Less than 20 minutes later, I checked his work. The first seven questions were perfect: answered *exactly* as they were supposed to be.

So I asked the class "Be honest. Nobody's judging you, least of all me: how many of you skimmed the story?"

Half of the class raised their hands.

"Okay, now keep your hands up if you had problems answering the questions."

Almost the same amount of students kept their hands up.

The problem that all of my "skimmers" were having was that 90% of my questions were contextual; not only was it a gauge of their comprehension…it was a gauge of their ability to reflect on the plight of Starla and her family.

They couldn't comprehend the questions (or apply them practically), because they had no ammo. By skimming, they looked for keywords to answer the question with. And failing that, they would just re-word the question.

John was one of six kids in my class that would automatically shoot his hand up, less than 10 minutes into a test, and say "Mr. Shaw? I don't understand this." It became a mantra. After the fifth time, I had one of my own.

"John? What's the question asking?"

Then, he'd re-read the question, mouthing it to himself (and sometimes aloud) and say "Ohhhh! Ok."

These "new" students are so enmeshed in trying to blast through tests quickly, that they don't stop to re-read when things are unclear.

And it isn't an isolated occurrence.

The very first day of every new semester, I give my students a pen and a questionnaire, with these directions:

THIS IS YOUR FIRST TEST! READ OVER THE ENTIRE TEST CAREFULLY BEFORE WRITING DOWN YOUR ANSWERS!

The test has 33 questions, including:

9.) Cross all words out on question #4

10.) List your three favorite ice cream flavors, in order of most to least favorite:

11.) Who would win in a fight, Superman or Batman? Explain.

12.) Clap five times. On the fifth time, say "HA!"

They'd get to the last question that was on the back of the paper, and it would read

33.) Only answer the first three questions. **Leave all others blank!** Each question answered after #3 will result in 10 points being deducted from your overall score. Students who have read the entire test and made NO marks on the test **after** question #3 will receive an A on their test, as well as a bonus test grade of 100%. Great Job!

Predictably, less than 10% of the classes would pass, and many would start the year with a negative grade. After the initial "test" I'd pass out the syllabus, which included a "student contract" detailing the class expectations, grading structure and class outline. The last paragraph read:

*By signing this contract, I'm certifying that I have read and understand all deadlines, test dates, expectations and grading systems. I will be held accountable for my own work, and will miss no more than three (3) assignments and three (3) quizzes in any one grading period. Occasionally I may request additional work for extra credit. This is not a guarantee of "free points," especially in the last weeks of class. Also, at any time, Mr. Shaw may remove one (1) but no more than (2) of my limbs with a chainsaw, to later sell on the dark web. This message may not be reproduced for any reason without the expressed permission of the national foosball league. If I agree to all **but** the chainsaw part, I will clearly mark an X after my name on the line below.*

If the students who took the *original* questionnaire got a "double F-minus," they could redeem themselves by placing an "X" after their name on the contract. That tells me that they're indeed learning from their mistakes. These students get the previous negative score expunged from their records, because they *should* have a reward for learning (at least, the second time around).

Without fail, though, I'll have another 10-15 students that *don't* have an "X" after their signature. These are my non-comprehenders. I will likely spend the next few months holding their hands and walking them through the minefield of school.

"But Mac," I can almost hear you asking, *"isn't that what a teacher is* supposed *to do?"*

Yes and no.

I'm here to instruct your kids on English, and ensure they take their tests well; when they test well, the school looks good. And when the school looks good, they keep getting that sweet, sweet revenue. So yes, your child is a commodity, not to put too fine of a point on it.

My main problem is that I simply *do not* feel comfortable sending a bunch of test-takers out into the world...because aside from college, the ability to bubble in a Scantron sheet deftly means jack shit to the rest of the world. And the only thing skimming does is help you finish a section of the New York Times in a single sitting.

Instead, they'll be "scanning" their first mortgage contract, their credit card applications (*"WHAT DO YOU MEAN 19% INTEREST! IT SAID ZERO IN THE COMMERCIAL!"*), EULAs for all of their social media and the fine print of their banking and cell phone contracts.

Some of the most important documents in their young lives will be signed *without ever being read*; at *best*, they'll get a cursory glance. *"After all, my banker/realtor/cellphone provider/Internet service provider/government knows best. I mean, why would they be in a nice suit, behind a mahogany desk if they* didn't *have my best interests in mind?!?"*

Add to that, many of my students have an IEP (individual education plan), which allow for a variety of accommodations, ranging from "extra time on a test" to "ability to leave class to talk with a counselor." But there's no weaning process for these services. Luckily, some students are working *while* they go to high school, and they'll soon realize that an IEP doesn't mean jack shit to their employer. For those who *don't* experience working until *after* they're out of high school, though, reality can be a stark slap in the face. After all, there's nothing quite as humbling as the first time you get fired for mouthing off to the wrong person.

These students are also part of a generation with both

parents working 40-50 hour work weeks (sometimes including weekends), so crucial information is often lost in the shuffle. Sure, some schools have "Home Ec"-type programs, but those classes still espouse the "making cookies/cake/bread and hand-stitching aprons/pillows" skillset. Meanwhile, the same students that will bake the hell out of a "from scratch" tray of brownies will still falter when confronted with balancing a basic household budget.

What about unclogging a drain? Replacing a blown fuse? Changing a flat tire? Routinely checking oil and tire pressure? Comparing bank statements? Addressing an envelope? Writing a resume, cover letter and a list of references? Creating a meal plan that balances the nutritional needs of your household? Knowing which cooking surfaces to bleach daily? How to sharpen a knife or start a fire? How many families have "go-bags" or know what to do in the event of an emergency? **Spoiler alert:** it's *shouldn't* be "sit tight and wait for the news to tell us what to do."

What we *do* train them to do is take tests effectively. We inspire mini-panic attacks by demanding that they take the PPSAT, the PSAT and the SAT (not to mention the horde of online "practice tests"). We teach them to skirt concepts like reason, understanding and comprehension by having them "seek out key terms" and parrot them back to us.

We "teach" by giving them packets to fill out. Instead of spending time explaining *why* something happens, we give them photocopied pictures and paragraphs and short-answer questions to ensure that they *actually* read and comprehend it.

Instead of inspiring them to self-motivate and explore our world, we spoon-feed them micro-modules that give them all the answers. We literally have a generation of the brightest, (and thanks to the internet) most well-informed young people, and instead of challenging them to take an active hand in changing their world, we tell them *"there will be time for that someday. For now, just take this quiz."*

Even with all that, there are still teachers who throw their shoulders against this "teaching" style: teachers who not only instruct, but inspire greatness in every student they encounter. Teachers who demand excellence and distill brilliance from the minds they fill with knowledge. Teachers who will lead these battalions of upstart classrooms into war against the "test-taking status quo." So, at least in *my* mind, all is not lost.

February 11th, 2014:

"A teachable moment"

Every single "problem" classroom I've been in has one thing in common: the illusion of control. At any given point, the class could rise up, en masse, and beat you to a weeping pulp. Some classrooms have an aide or two to stop this from happening, but most only have a radio; failing that, a phone. And the response time to most phone calls is three to five minutes. Not exactly the lightning quick response you'd expect.

The only way to mitigate such problems is to command the room. Period. From the second you walk in, to the second you leave, you're on stage. You'll be ignored if you're not interesting, engaging or relevant. If you immediately put a desk between you and the rowdy masses, you're pretty much admitting that you're scared…at least a little bit. It makes sense, since "public speaking" often lands in the top 5 fears of most people.

For these students, fear is just blood in the water… and it's only a matter of time before the sharks start circling. Luckily for me, as a former "bad kid," I'm pretty well versed on fleecing people, and I tend to be a fast learner in the event of a slip up.

If a student can get one over on me, I'll usually reward them; hell, that's one more entry in my already extensive "Ledger of Malfeasance." But when students try to come through with a sub standard scam, that's when the fun really begins.

Without fail, word travels quickly through the school hallways, and by the second week of the semester, when I walk in the room, kids know what side their toast is buttered on. If they don't, their friends will usually pull them in line. Sometimes they won't…and sometimes they let them crash and burn purely for entertainment.

Take, for example, Thuggsley: one of the new additions to the "recidivist" school I was assigned to for a month. The kid was the very definition of a "try hard": he was a 5'2 chubby blonde kid who punctuated nearly every sentence with "n***a" and would trail off after ending with "fuckin' I dunno." He came from a fairly affluent suburb that bordered on rural, and instead of working on his family farm, he spent his time "plugging motherfuckers in Call of Duty."

One morning he strolled into class 15 minutes late, interrupting the lecture on the Fall of Rome. He shuffled past me, one hand clutched above his gut, twisting his hoodie. It doesn't take me long to realize that he's emulating some rapper, but instead of grabbing his crotch, he's grabbing his sweatshirt. I think you might have missed the mark there, super chieftain.

From the minute he sits down, his mouth doesn't stop running. He's yammering about the "fire weed" he has, his uncle that's "totally, like a (gang)banger

126

that's in, like witness protection" *and how* "bitches are on his dick 24/7. No, like, really!" *None of the other students are impressed…but like hyenas, they're smiling, waiting for me to light into him. I suggest that he stop talking and disrupting the class, and he does…for a second. Then he's right back to* "gettin' drunk and fuckin' fighting." *I continue on with my lecture, knowing that 90 of the class is following along.*

Thuggsley doesn't seem to take the hint.

He bookends every one of his outrageous claims with a furtive glance around the room, to see if he's getting a rise out of anyone. A few times he mentions a popular rap song, and after seeing another student nod, he goes full bore into "how (insert rapper here) is the sickest spitter alive."

The other kids just roll their eyes. I don't even bother lighting into him, since he'll be out of this program in a couple of weeks, back to his primarily white school, where he won't have to glance around before saying "n***a."

But I don't let it go, either.

Instead, I keep a tally sheet nearby, with an uppercase F, N, D and M listed. Next to each is a series of marks.

At the end of class, I send him home with a sealed envelope addressed to his mother, containing the tally sheet and the following letter:

Dear Mrs. (Thuggsley),

Today, during his Social Sciences class, your son arrived 15 minutes late. That in itself isn't a big deal, but he spent the rest of the class period loudly attempting to engage his peers in conversation, though both myself and his fellow students asked him to stop.

In those conversations, he used the words "n***a" no less than 37 times, "fuck" more than 50 times (in various iterations), "biches all over his dick" 6 times, and loudly advertised that he had "fire weed (high quality marijuana) that he's looking to sell, and that his parents are too dumb to find" (p.s. it's apparently in his closet, in his baseball glove), and "how he's been replacing the vodka in your liquor cabinet with water after making 'Faderade' (a mixture of vodka and Gatorade)" which he then supposedly drinks on the bus.

This was all during one class period. I checked his notebook and project work. He did not complete any of it. I'm attaching printouts of the project for him to work on tonight.

I'm also CCing the email address you have on file, in the event that this doesn't make its way to you. If possible, please sign and date the bottom so I know you've read it?

Best,

M.C. Shaw

P.S. Today's lecture was on accountability, so if he delivers this letter to you, unopened, and brings it back signed by you (and with today's work), he'll receive two bonus A grades this week, for being accountable. Forgeries and modified letters will receive four F's.

See? Not all lessons in my classroom are taught in my classroom.

I'll bet dollars to doughnuts that he'll be singing a different tune when he comes in tomorrow. After all, there's only so much I can do to penalize him in class. But at home? He's about to enter a whole new level of agony.

The best part? He'll be sure to bemoan his treatment in my classes to the other kids at lunchtime, and that's one less life lesson I'll have to preach from my lectern.

Chapter 11:

"The Rarity Of Amazing Teachers"

I know it's a bit of a shit thing to say, but I can honestly say that in my entire time spent as a student, I can count the great teachers I've had on one hand. I've had plenty of good teachers, and a couple dozen mediocre "teachers"... and a whole mess of flat out terrible ones.

I think the biggest problem with teaching is the problem with most jobs: people get stuck in a rut, and though they may have loved that job at the beginning, later they don't really give much of a shit about doing a good job anymore. They're content with literally and figuratively photocopying their annual lesson without innovation, eking out a paycheck with the mantra of "because what *else* am I gonna do?"

A good teacher will make you pay attention in class...but a *great* teacher will challenge your preconceptions about learning, and make you excited to come to class each day. Great teachers chase the high of connecting new and exciting material with their kids, and end up fulfilled as a result.[13]

In fifth grade, I had one of the best teachers I've ever had in my life: Mrs. Reap. She was one of those people who just *understood* kids; she always had an impish smile on her face and a sparkle in her eyes. She was like Mrs. Frizzle crossed with your favorite grandmother, and she *totally* "got" me.

Fifth grade was an especially important year in my development, because it was the first time I was ever given an IQ test--and the first time I was ever labeled as "neurologically different." Sure, the testing showed that I was in the 98th percentile in terms of knowledge acquisition and application, but that wasn't all.

Though it wasn't really something as widely diagnosed today, ADHD was something that sent many parents running for the hills (or to the closest pharmacy) in the 80s. I was lucky enough to have a school psychiatrist that was more interested in the "why" of the diagnosis, and suggested giving me a different academic option instead of just treating it with meds.

Mrs. Reap was totally onboard with this, and suggested giving me movement breaks, and letting me choose where I wanted to sit. I opted for a seat in the back corner of the room, immediately adjacent to the door so I could pop in and out when I needed to move around. She also allowed me to complete work at my own pace, and if I finished the day's work early, I could read quietly. These were the golden years of the BOOK IT! program, where you could earn a personal pan pizza from Pizza Hut if you read three books and wrote a single-page report on them. I earned more than 25 personal pan pizza coupons that year, and almost single-handedly won a pizza party for our class from the sheer number of book reports I logged.

I didn't have another truly great teacher again until 8th grade when I had Mr. Lambert, a barrel-shaped, soft-spoken man who taught us that Shakespeare was meant to be *experienced*...not just read. He shared his love of Poe and Ray Bradbury and above all, loved books almost as much as he loved his family. He was the first teacher that made us realize that teachers were actually *people* and even more than that--that it was okay to be fallible. He would model vulnerability and would say things like "you know what? I don't know the answer to that. But I'll look into it and tell you tomorrow." And it would be his first order of business the following day. This was in stark contrast to many teachers that would blatantly make shit up, or change the subject when confronted with something they didn't know.

He was also the first teacher to tell us that it's okay to be scared when speaking publicly, and go on to tell us about the things that still scared him. He was one of the most *human* teachers I've ever had, and had that amazing ability to turn "wrong" answers into "right" conversations, by saying things like "I think I see where you were going there...and you're almost there! It's a little closer to *this*." Thereby honoring the thought process behind the student's attempt, while guiding them closer to the correct answer.

That same year, I had a religious studies teacher named Miss Mill, who had the letters PBUTC inscribed over her chalkboard-- it stood for "Personal Best Under The Circumstances." If you bombed a test because you slept like crap, or were stressed about something at home, you could set a meeting with her and plead your case. Chances were that she would let you retake it, or come up with an alternate assignment to make up the points--as long as you didn't take advantage of her kindness.

In 9th grade, I had another incredible religious studies teacher named Father Dan; a wiry, whippet-skinny madman who was as insane as he was brilliant. He had an incredible knack for incorporating absurdist statements and behavior into what might be otherwise dry and boring material. Though he was a priest, he would tell students that he was an alien from another planet...and some of us believed him. In the back of his classroom, there was a picture of him where he weighed, conservatively, 300 lbs and was wearing a sweater vest. When we would ask him about it, he'd smile and say "that was the first vessel that they gave me when I landed on this planet. It didn't work well for me, so they saw fit to send me another." He would also stand with his nose to the chalkboard at the front of his room, with his eyes closed, and hum. When we would ask him what he was doing, he would smirk and say "I'm tuning my body's frequency to this wall so I'll be able to pass through it." Later that day, we'd see him leaving the classroom next door, and he'd smile and say "It WORKED!"

One of the best qualities of Father Dean was that he was bombastic in his vocabulary and his volume, and if you were in his presence, you couldn't help but pay attention. If a student said "I don't know" he would counter with "YES YOU *DO*, CHILD OF GOD AND HEIR TO THE KINGDOM! I BELIEVE IN YOUR ABILITY TO RECOLLECT!" And then he would give hints and prompts until they were back on track. By leading a single student to the answer, all of us would learn as well. When you would pepper your answer with "like," as in "the story we read is, like, one of the..." he would interject "THE STORY WE READ IS 'LIKE' NOTHING IN THE WORLD, CHILD! IT *IS* AND THEREFORE YOU WILL TREAT IT AS SUCH!" The man single-handedly struck the idea of punctuating "like" from our formal answers without belittling or mocking; he simply reinforced the truth of what words meant.

My absolute favorite memory of Father Dan, however, was when I was having a loud disagreement in the hallway with two of my classmates. I was shooting my mouth off, and we had started shoving each other, when from behind us, we heard the voice of the Metatron.

"What is going on here, *GENTLEMENNNN?!*" His voice started

as a whisper, and ended in a thundering roar. He pointed at his room, and we all filed in, eyes downcast. He shut the door behind us. "Now, what were you *just* talking about?"

All of us mumbled something along the lines of "nothing." He smiled, pushed his glasses up on his nose and said "Interesting. Because I distinctly recall hearing young mister Shaw say *'if any of you motherfuckers want to swing on me, you should stop talking shit and fucking do it.'* Or was I mistaken?"

We were all flabbergasted. No teacher had ever so quietly and politely called us out on our bullshit, much less repeated our own terrible language back to us. We left his room acutely aware that he had us dead to rights, yet none of us got detention that day. He just wanted us to know that *he* knew we were full of shit.

Great teachers *listen.*

I'm as guilty as the next person when it comes to actively listening. Sure, a bunch of it is my ADHD, but it's really difficult not to listen with an agenda. One of my first high school girlfriends said something like "the best kind of people are the ones who listen...not the ones who wait to talk." And even though it's trite, it's true. Once you start listening, *really* listening to your students, you begin to build an actual connection with them.

Every single one of the "great" teachers I've had the honor of working alongside all have one thing in common: an honest and sincere wish to create meaningful relationships with students. I mean, to be a good teacher, all you *really* need to do is give a shit about your students and *actually* mean it. But great teachers are on a whole different level; great teachers have meaningful relationships as the bedrock of their teaching...especially when you're working with students who have emotional needs and/or challenges with self-regulation. Just letting them know you hear them can be the first step in building rapport.

I overheard an amazing exchange while waiting for one of my co-teachers who happened to be working at an elementary school. A little girl, no more than eight, comes out of the front doors rubbing her eyes, clearly upset. Her dad was standing by the flagpole as she walked up to him, dragging her feet the whole way. He knelt down to tie her shoe and said "looks like something's bugging you." He held up three fingers, "Do you want me to tell you how to fix it?" He put one finger down, "Do you want me to ask questions until you figure out how to fix it yourself?" He put down another finger, "Or do you just want to vent?"

"I just wanna vent," she said sniffling. Turns out that some jerk named Kelly knocked over her watercolor cup AGAIN during art, and it ruined her picture. Dad suggested something to her, but I couldn't hear...mostly because I didn't want to be the creepy ex-felon-looking guy eavesdropping on their conversation.

But seriously, though: that interaction has stuck with me all these years, and whenever I approach a conversation with a student, I try to actively listen (which can be a feat in and of itself) and offer the three choices when they come to me with a problem. It reinforces that they're in control of how we handle it, but also gives them a chance to be heard.

That extends to my lesson planning as well: I like to co-create my lessons with the students whenever possible. I can't tell you how many times I start building out a lesson, only to discover that a third of the class are missing the key foundational skills that *my* lesson is based on. Plus, by asking for and implementing student feedback, they actually feel like they have a vested interest in the learning process.

You wouldn't believe the incredible things I've learned about students by paying attention to their conversations and checking in with them. One of the biggest challenges for me is using neutral language when talking with kids. Like, instead of saying "why are you falling asleep in class!?" I've since adopted "I feel" or "I notice" phrasing, like "I noticed that it was hard for you to stay awake in class today. What's going on?"

Great teachers *notice*.

I know I'm beating a dead horse here, but *always* keep a secret stash of granola bars and shelf-stable snacks in your desk. You can't imagine how many students I've had over the years that are up at 3 and 4 in the morning just to get ready and be at school on time. Or how many kids are responsible for feeding, dressing and getting their younger siblings to school. Or how many parents refuse to fill out the Free and Reduced Lunch documents as a matter of pride, and how that trickles down to the kids not wanting to be known as "handout kids." So I always keep a mini pantry of shelf-stable food locked in my drawers, as well as a couple of extra clean tee-shirts, hoodies, and socks in one of those Rubbermaid totes under my desk.

A few years back I noticed that one of my students, Tim, wore the same outfit to class four days in a row, and both the clothes and the kid were getting progressively dingier. I found out that he was living out of a car with his mom and little sister. Mom was afraid to say anything to anyone, for fear of being labeled as neglectful. That afternoon, I picked up a bottle of dry shampoo, three sticks of deodorant, and a bunch of granola bars, and put them inside a brown paper bag, stapled it and hid it under my desk. I asked Tim if he could help me out with a survey after class, and once the kids all filtered out, I gave him the bag. I told him it wasn't pity or charity, but to think of it as a loan that he could pay to someone else later in life. I also gave him one of my super plush hoodies, since it was winter and I didn't know how much longer they'd be without a house. That same kid later graduated high school with a 3.8 GPA and enrolled in college, in a program to become a licensed clinical social worker.

"Noticing" also works for challenging kids in your classes too! I can't tell you how many times I was able to help redirect a "problem" student just by telling them things I noticed about them. So many kids feel like they're background characters in some generic high school movie, and sometimes just pointing out that you can *see* them can be enough to bring them back to the fold.

Defusing frustrated kids can be as easy as walking up to them and quietly saying "I feel like you might be hitting a wall. Did you want to take a quick three-minute break and walk around?" and then either walk *with* them or check back in with them when they return.

I have a kiddo with some major behavioral challenges, but he's also been one with whom I've worked hardest all year. He has huge challenges with blurting inappropriate things and perspective taking with other students (and adults) resulting in lots of misunderstandings and frustrating exchanges. When it was getting towards the end of the school year, I told him that if he had three solid "good communication" weeks in a row, I'll buy him any size/combination of Cold Stone ice cream he wanted (and that shit is *expensive*).

Five minutes before the last bell, we would check in and review his interactions for the day. He managed to get through three weeks with full points...and then stumbled on the last day. He's a kid that needs to follow a rigorous schedule, and on that day there was a sudden deviation from it, which made him snap at his tablemates. After taking a break walking around with him, I told him that I'd consider the bad day to be a mulligan, and if he knocked it out of the park the following day, I'd still honor our bet. Unsurprisingly, he absolutely crushed it.

After school that day, I walked him to Cold Stone and helped him read the flavors (he has a couple processing challenges), and he loudly declared that he would "have a vanilla latte!" while pointing at the tub labeled "Vanilla Lite." And when she handed him his scoops, I didn't even need to prompt him to say "please and thank you" to the server. He even asked her how her day was going! Major progress! However, he had yet to say anything like "thank you" to me.

As we walked back to school, I turned to him and said "I noticed how awesomely polite you were to the server in there, and even asked her info exchange questions like 'what's your favorite mix-in and why?' Killer work! Now is there anything you want to say to me?"

He took a pensive spoonful of his ice cream, then looked me dead in the eye and said "yes. I'm pretty sure this is called 'favoritism.'"

I narrowed my eyes at him, and he cackled loud enough to startle the crows in the nearby tree.

March 14th, 2013:

"Love is an awkward battlefield"

Ok, so today I had the incredible fortune of working with students who require a bit of additional time and patience. They're awesome, incredibly gifted in areas, and genuinely fantastic to be around. No lie.

The school I was at had 11th grade testing all day, and when students finished up their exams, they were pretty much free agents; IE, they could go home, stay at school, etc.

One such free agent, let's call him Jeff (obviously not his real name) drops into the classroom, and very politely asks

"Um…Mr. S? Would it, uh, be ok if I, uh, stayed in here to work on my homework? My Dad isn't going to pick me up until 3, so I'm stuck, and…"

Without hearing anymore, I immediately said yes. After all, the kid was polite enough to seek me out, learn my name and request to stay. Absolutely no worries.

Let me describe Jeff: he's a 17 year old, skinny, socially awkward teen with acne, clothing of the Hot

Topic variety, and long, stringy blond hair with Kool Aid color streaks. Got a visual? Good.

He sits on the floor cross legged, and I immediately ask if he'd like to sit at a desk (as several were available).

"No thank you, Mr. S. I like being closer to the earth."

Again, totally shocked by his politeness, I move on to other students. About 10 minutes later, I saw one of my female students cautiously approaching him.

"Penny" is also 17 with ripped jean shorts over her tights, Chuck Taylors, a Black Flag shirt (immediate gold star status in my classroom), and a safety pin DIY hoodie with several punk bands I've never heard of. But whatever. She's "punk pretty" with a sweet, polite disposition...and has blonde hair with bright red streaks.

I realize that I'm about to see the budding courtship of nu metal/Hot Topic punks in action. I settle in, like a documentarian watching the rituals of some forgotten Amazonian tribe.

Penny: Uh...Jeff?

Jeff: Yeah?

P: Um...you don't have to sit on the floor. I mean, if you want to that's, like, awesome or whatever. But there's seats all around the room, and there's...uh... (she stares at her shoes)

J: What are you saying?

P: (flustered) Uh...I'm just saying that if you

wanted, there's, like, an open seat over by…me?

Now, at this point, I'm holding my breath so I don't let out an "AWWWWWWWWWWWWWWWWEEEEEE" and disturb the adorkable moment that's happening.

Then, like the index finger of an angry god, Jeff explodes, pointing his finger into Penny's face.

"Don't you think I can see what you're trying to do!? You just go back over there and sit down! PUT ALL OF THAT BEING FLIRTY AWAY! RIGHT NOW! GO FIND SOMEONE ELSE TO KISS ALL OVER BECAUSE THAT PERSON ISN'T ME! I'M DOING HOMEWORK!"

It took about seven strips of duct tape to fix my jaw, after it crashed to the floor.

"Penny" went back to her seat, nearly in tears, and sat quietly. Minutes later when I checked on her, she had a huge smile on her face and showed us her high score on Angry Birds.

There's something fantastic to say about the resilience of youth…especially neuroatypical kids. I wish all kids had that inner strength.

As far as Jeff? I got nothin' for that kid.

Well, that's not true: I asked him if he would like to have been treated like that. He replied with a glum "no" and went back to drawing a maze on his notebook.

Before the bell rang, he walked over and apologized to Penny, unprompted, and gave her an "apology high five."

Nice. The kids are (mostly) alright.

Chapter 12:

"A Condemnation Of Awful Teachers"

Working in an educational system with as diverse a population as I do, you're bound to run into a few "problem people." Funny thing is, even though I have my share of challenging students, the majority of issues I ran into over the past 10 years were with other teachers.

But let's go back even further--my first experience with a genuinely *bad* teacher was in second grade. Mrs. Bannon was a skinny but sloppy woman with long, dry silver and black hair. I remember her having these ridiculous bags under her eyes, and spots of dark skin all over her face and arms, like she spent too much time in the sun without sunscreen. She had a habit of sneering when she spoke, and would call kids up to the front of the classroom to dress them down in front of everyone for the slightest infraction. Draw your letters wrong? Front of the class. Not wash your hands long enough? Front of the class. Tie your shoes with the "bunny loop" and not the "over-under"? Front of the class for a heaping helping of humiliation.

I was a kid that read faster upside down instead of right side up, and nothing bothered her more than non-compliance. It was so bad that I'd read with my book in my lap so she wouldn't catch me. I was a frequent flier when it came to "front of the classroom" trips, and she'd send letters home to my parents weekly. This was also the first time that I had anything less than an S (for satisfactory) in all subjects. There wasn't a day that went by that she didn't go out of her way to make me feel like a big dumb box of shit.

One thing that sticks out most in my mind was a "class activity" that we did during the winter of that year. On the first day of December, we all got a mimeograph of a snowman with numbered blank spots on him, like a cheap advent calendar. If you had a "good day" you were given a cotton ball and a bottle of Elmer's Glue and allowed to add a cotton ball to your snowman. By the end of the month, most kids had a fluffy, smiling snowman tacked to the wall; I had a post-apocalyptic monstrosity, with three fluff balls on his torso from the days that we had a substitute. The rest of my poor snowman looked like something from Gray's Anatomy, with pale dotted blue lines and a series of numbers down his body--not something to take home and put on the fridge. Each day, she would point my snowman out to the other kids, and say "see? You don't want to end up with a snowman like MacArthur's...*do you?*"

At the first (and only) parent-teacher meeting that year, Mrs. Bannon spent the entire time telling my parents how useless and ineffective I was, and "how she could try to explain what was wrong with me in teacher terms, but since my parents were so wholly intellectually inept when it came to the ins and outs of classroom structures, it wouldn't really do any good." Mind you, my mom was a classroom teacher for years, and *her* mother was a career teacher. My dad taught his sisters to read, and helped them with their homework from grade school through graduation.

My mother still hasn't told me what she screamed at Ms. Bannon, but apparently it frightened her so much that she left the room, and refused to return until my parents were out of the hallway.

I'm probably breaking some "double-super-secret-silent teacher code" by saying this, but much like the people you encounter daily, not all teachers are inherently *good*; in fact, most are mediocre...or worse.

Before I qualify that statement, I'll be the first to put myself in the crosshairs:

Sure, I have a student population where 80% think I'm the bees knees, coupled with a positive track record whilst in long-term classrooms, and all of my students have exhibited continuous positive academic and social growth.

But.

I can also be abrasive, loud, dismissive and judgmental at times.

When simple directions are repeatedly unheeded by an entire class (or worse, by a teacher or administrator), I get frustrated and have the world's worst poker face. That being said, while wearing my "teacher's hat" on campus, I never use profanity or resort to overzealous punishment methods. And I've *never* made an example out of someone who hasn't had numerous chances to mend their ways.

I'm a huge believer in a person's ability to change--but sometimes, they need a mirror held up to them, in order to see that a change might be necessary in the first place.

When I first started subbing, I was as doe-eyed as they come. Luckily (or not, depending on how you look at it), the first district after Scout's that I was assigned to was, arguably, one of the hardest in the state.

For me, the biggest problem was transitioning into the "normal" districts, after a year of living life on the edge. One of the first "normal" schools I worked at after Lil' Shawshank was a snooty, upper-class "academy," with a group of kids who thought they were hard...and teachers who did too.

Day 1, some other teacher *ate my lunch*, drank half of my bottle of water, and my coffee vanished entirely. When I asked around, I was told that it was likely "sub hazing" and not to take it personally. Keep in mind, subs make about a third of the daily take that a teacher does; long term subs get a little more, but not much. So "sub hazing" is just a shitty way of saying "I'm a lazy piece of shit teacher who decided to eat *your* lunch instead of buying my own."

Add to that, at least once a week, I'd either get called or emailed to pick up a job for a teacher, only to arrive at the school and discover that the teacher "placed their friend on the assignment instead" and failed to update the sub system.

Even worse, I'd have teachers who would slot me in for a full-day assignment, but when I got to the site, I'd find out that they only taught a single class period. One of the tenured teachers at that school told me that the teachers do that, "because most subs won't show up if they list the 'real' hours." Neat.

So, instead of a full day's pay, you get an hour's worth. And, by accepting that assignment, you're ineligible to accept another job at a different location that same day.

Not to mention the repetitive list of teachers that would call out sick because they were hung over, and the students (likely children of alcoholics) were painfully aware "of why Ms. Baskine always wears sunglasses indoors...even when it's dark outside."

Eventually, all of these things coalesce and can temper your exasperation into something...*darker.*

Way back at Scout's school, there was a teacher named Mr. Neff who was abrupt and dismissive with me from the jump. He was known as "the cool teacher" on campus. He would often use flippant profanity in his classrooms, show R-rated films that had little to do with the subject matter and generally go overboard in pursuit of deification from his students.

He was a squat, swarthy man, with frizzy black hair and a patchy beard that never *quite* came in evenly. He made up for this with a massive *"look at me, I'm the cool guy"* complex, but never had the actual presence to pull it off. But he said "fuck" and "shit" all the time, so the kids loved him.

After the first week or so, word had gotten around to him that there might have been a challenger to the "fun teacher" throne... and he wasn't having any of it.

Predictably, the students were eating it up, and used every possible chance to compare him to me, to goad him into some sort of dust-up.Though I love to bask in adoration (and really, who doesn't?), I don't actually seek it out. If people hate me? Great. If they love me? Well, that's super neato too.

I like having open dialogues with my students, but I couldn't care less about why they dislike me, so long as they do their work and respect the rules...and each other.

Back to Neff: during the fifth week of my long-term assignment, there was a shortage of staff on campus. Some of the smaller classes ended up getting combined, so teachers and their students would be sharing one big room. First thing Monday morning, I got my assignment: I'd be sharing my room with Mr. Neff for the week.

Immediately, students started whispering. Apparently, Mr. Neff got his room assignment on Friday, and spent the morning voicing his displeasure to his own students.

How professional.

And now, my kids were doing everything except whispering *"FIGHT! FIGHT! FIGHT! FIGHT!"* every time we were in the same area.

Instead of feeding into the fervor, I remained quiet. After taking attendance, I gathered my ducklings and headed toward Neff's room. As the kids got settled, I heard him say "...aaaaaand he's late. What a surprise." His students tittered.

He powered up the projector and readied the day's powerpoint presentation, I began to set up my laptop, file folders and gradebook.

At *his* desk.

It was a good five minutes before he realized what was happening.

"Excuse me...*what are you doing*?" Instantly, the classroom became silent.

I looked up from the notebook. "I'm transferring grades. Go ahead and start the presentation. I'm good!"

"What? Oh...ok."

I spent the whole presentation taking cursory notes (to later quiz my students), and keeping to myself. As the class wound down, he shut off the ancient projector and reset the presentation for his next class. I gathered up my things as the kids milled around, ready to stream out into the halls.

"Great class today, Neff!"

He looked up from the laptop. "I know."

"It would mean the world to me if you could keep the desktop clear during our shared periods."

"What? But that's my..."

"When I'm here, it's *my* desk."

"Yeah, but…"

"Great. Thank you *soooooooo* much." I smiled a huge Stepford smile and strolled out of the room.

The kids witnessed the entire exchange, and I won the battle without having to fire a single shot. The next day, he intentionally left his things all over the desk. So I just set up everything *on top* of his papers, and ran my class as usual. Whenever he'd grumble about not being able to get to his papers, I would cheerily remind him "if he had just kept the shared workspace clear, *he wouldn't be in this frustrating position.*"

Sometimes the path of least resistance can be the most satisfying.

I've also heard substitute teachers explicitly talk down to students as if they were puppies at a shelter. Many of the "older" subs seemingly cannot differentiate between "exceptional needs" and "comatose" so they just talk to all the kids with disabilities like they're infants.

One classroom had two students with cerebral palsy who were academically classified as "advanced," but had homeroom in a class with other students with exceptionally high needs. There were also a couple students with auditory processing issues, two students in wheelchairs and another girl who had to take walking breaks every half hour to self-regulate. The first time I worked in that room, it was daunting; but then I read the teacher's notes, and everything went swimmingly.

Unfortunately, the other co-teacher substitute did *not* read the class notes, and actually got incensed when I quietly suggested she do so. Not only did it give descriptors and individual info on each student, it also explicitly said to let them work independently unless they ask for assistance.

Instead of heeding the directions (which, to be fair, she didn't read), she decided to be literally "hands-on" with them, whether they wanted help or not.

The co-substitute seemed to have two modes: "normal" and "sickeningly sweet 1/4 speed" when talking to one of the students who had cerebral palsy, she grasped both of his shoulders like an preacher at a tent revival and yelled

"RIIIIIIIIIIIICH-AAAAARD! DOOOOOO YOOOOOOOUUUU KNOOOOOOOOOW HOOOWWWW TOOOOOO FIIIII-NIIIIIISHHH THIIIIIIIIS PRRRR-AHHHHH-JECT?!"

He rolled his eyes at her, and answered "Yes...I got it. No...problem."

Unfortunately, his hitching delivery seemed to confirm that she was addressing him in the correct tone. This continued every time she spoke to him (or the other student with cerebral palsy), and she used the same approach for the guy in the wheelchair. Yet, when talking to the student with auditory processing issues, she gave direction at full speed ("because she *looked* normal"), and would get annoyed when the girl couldn't keep up. Watching this unfold felt like someone was jabbing my brain with a shiv, and every time I tried to interject helpfully, I was dismissed with a wave.

She didn't last long, especially when the kids gave a scathing report to the classroom teacher upon her return, which resulted in the teacher requesting that I cover all of her future absences.

The absolute worst co-sub experience, however, was a doddering-yet-creepy older sub...let's call him Mr. Rex. He was an older man, somewhere between 55 and 70, with a short stocky body that made him look like a giant, bespectacled baby.

When he wasn't dozing off at his desk, Mr. Rex spent the remainder of his day walking up and down the aisles, leering at the teenage girls in the classroom; his rheumy, owlish eyes creeping up their leggings and down their low-cut tops. He didn't even attempt to mask his intentions, and he would stare with his mouth hung open, corners smeared with white, dried saliva.

Unfortunately, the real show began at lunch. Since it was my first day at that particular school, I wasn't well-versed on where the mythical staff lounge was...and seeing as how we only had 30 minutes to eat lunch and prep for the following class, I couldn't waste time exploring.

The classroom shared an accordion-style partition, and while I closed and locked my classroom's outer doors at lunchtime, Mr. Rex decided to invite students into his room, and threw the partition open "to give everyone more room." He then sidled up to my desk, and decided that I would be his lunch buddy.

Since we were "buddies," he spent half of the lunch break fondly recounting his adoration for Marilyn Chambers[14] to me, marveling at how she could "accommodate almost anything...*at either end!*" Sure, he never expressly said "fucked" or "blew" or "jerked," but it was enough to make me uncomfortable...and

150

more than a little nauseous. When I told him to stop, because he was in earshot of the kids, he started using more vague terminology.

Unfortunately, these were high school kids, not a pack of brain-dead goats. Yes, they understand what you're saying, and if they don't know the vocabulary, they'll easily suss out your meaning, either from context, or from your creepy, oily tone (not to mention his "*nudge-nudge-wink-wink*" eyebrow waggling).

Look, I get it: I look like someone you'd find in an adult theater at noon on a Tuesday...but I'm really *not* that guy. What I *am*, is incredibly well aware of what **can** and **can't** be discussed in a classroom. And 70s porn, no matter how veiled or reverent the description, is right the fuck out.

Plus, I don't want to imagine your tiny, veiny baby hands doing the five knuckle shuffle over reel-to-reel stag porn as you wistfully recount "the first time you ever saw a scene with her."

When he wasn't lauding the physical achievements of Ms. Chambers, he would loudly fill me in on his stance on "NO-Bama" and how "his name was an acronym for One Big Ass Mistake for America," how "illegal immigration will be our downfall," how "he met Hannity once on his speaking tours" and how "Ted Nugent is the ultimate man's man...but not in that *gay* way."

If he was any more dated and two-dimensional, he would have come with bad lighting and a laugh track.

At the end of that day, I reported him to the secretary, since there was nothing to be gained from dressing him down in public. And to be honest, I doubt he'd even have the wits to be ashamed. Yet, when I mentioned his actions, the other teachers just laughed and said "yup...that's Mr. Rex being Mr. Rex."

Apparently, Rex was known far and wide for being a screw-off, and was treated with the same affinity as an old dog that spends his days napping and barking at nothing. Sure, sometimes he shits all over the rug...but he's *ooooooooooold* and has been here *fooooo-revvvvvver*. Apparently, "too old to know better" is a fair defense when confronted with the question of putting him out to pasture.

I'd love to say that was the last time I ever encountered him, but it wasn't. It got to the point where he would approach me smirking, and I'd loudly bark "NOPE!" Eventually, he got the idea.

Conversely, I've gone to bat for teachers who were railroaded by shitty kids. Last year, I had overheard a fairly bookish, grandfatherly-type teacher snap, and say "I am *NOT* a f*ggot, you *JACKASS!*" at a mouthy, 17-year-old wannabe Supreme gangsta.

Apparently, the kid was throwing balls of paper and baiting him for the better part of 20 minutes, and on his way out of the classroom, he said *"fuckin' old f*g. Go fuck yourself"* under his breath, as he shoulder-checked the sub. I caught the tail end of the exchange.

After getting yelled at, the mouthy rich boy tried to say that he "was gonna get that old bitch fired," and word got around to the other students.

So it was a surprising turn of events when I submitted a suspension report about how "the student repeatedly bullied the smaller teacher, threw objects at him, used hate speech and physically assaulted him by pushing him into a door."

When the kid tried to say that the teacher yelled profanity at him, I went on record saying that I couldn't recall anything of the sort occurring. Plus, I may have suggested that students who overheard him spread disinformation among their peers. He didn't say "jackass"...he said "scamp." Or "ruffian." Or "buster." Or, my personal favorite, "ham-fisted clown." As a result, witnesses had mysteriously conflicting reports, and no solid punishment was able to be levied against the elderly sub.

All things considered, I've definitely worked with more good teachers than bad, and of the good ones, several have been exceptional. Granted, the bad ones have been horrible, but the great ones have been absolutely inspiring.

Sure, a big part of being a teacher is instinctual, but the remaining ability is cobbled together from all of the fantastic educator styles I've witnessed, as well as the vast variety of students I've worked with.

At the end of the day, even the worst teachers can still be a benchmark, and they can be crystal clear examples of what you *don't* want to do. And on the upside, at 4 p.m., no matter how awful they are, I still get to go home to my amazing life...while they get to go home to Hot Pockets , a plastic jug of Evan Williams and crippling self-doubt.

April 18th, 2013:

"Because we are so very pretty…"

The school I was working at today had a lockdown drill. I guess in the past, administrators would tell teachers, who would then tell their students (great job!) and nobody would react to the drill. Throughout the alarm, they would just continue on like nothing happened, or simply do something to entertain their students during the distraction.

There was an ACTUAL lockdown at this school a few months back, and people were reacting like it was another stupid drill. Result? Kids milling around, talking on their cell phones and generally being apathetic. You know: the usual.

So this time, the administrators triggered the alarm without telling anyone.

If you're unfamiliar, the lockdown procedure is this:

When the alarm goes off, you're supposed to tell all nearby students to GET INTO THE CLASSROOM. Once you've cleared the hall, you draw the blinds, lock the doors and turn off the lights. Students and teachers are both told to sit on the ground, preferably with their backs to something bulletproof, away from doors and windows, and behind a desk if possible.

Then, they are instructed to be as quiet as possible

to give the illusion that the classroom is empty.

Students are then told NOT TO ANSWER THE DOOR FOR ANY REASON...even if the people who knock say that they're police, since any real LEOs would have a skeleton key to clear the rooms.

In a standard high school classroom, this would be challenging. Especially the whole "keeping quiet part."

Today's drill happened when I was subbing in a Moderate/Severely Emotional Disturbed classroom. On a normal day, teaching a class like that is akin to herding a flock of ornery cats into a single vet bound carrier.

Today, it was like herding cats into a cage while A SCREAMING, GRATING ALARM WAS WAILING IN THE BACKGROUND. Once we locked the doors and shut off the lights, the tapping, kicking, whimpering and giggling began. After finally getting them to quiet down to an absolute silence (5 to 10 minutes worth of gradual, tedious work), the administrators/police decided to take the lockdown test further by banging on the door and yelling OPEN UP!

That reignited the whimpers and nervous ticking, which we moved to quiet, when a girl looked up at me, eyes all teary, and asked

"Mister? Are we going to die today?"

You know that "teacher teleprompter"? The one that has all the right responses to the easy questions? Yeah, I had nothing. Her words deleted everything on my mental script. I couldn't think of a single "right thing" to say that wouldn't come across as *condescending.*

Then it hit me. In a calm, strong whisper, I said

"We are NOT going to die today. And do you know why? Because we are so… very… pretty. Too pretty for it to end like this." I pointed at my chin "Look at this gorgeous beard and chiseled jaw, huh? Nothing bad's gonna happen. Not today! Not to us! *Way* too pretty!"

The girl grinned (as did a couple of her classmates), and the tears slowly vanished.

Thanks, Mal.

Chapter 13:

"Shit Admin In Need Of A Double Flush"

Nothing hamstrings a potentially amazing teacher quite like bad administration. I've been extremely lucky in my time being a substitute teacher; in that, I was able to observe multiple examples of shit-tier admin, and it was incredible what I'd overheard given that I wasn't a "real" teacher.

As a substitute, the principal's secretary can either be your best friend...or your worst enemy. Hell, at a couple of assignments, they ended up being both! They tend to be a little freer with their words, but are quick to throw teachers and staff under the bus. Of course, when you're the substitute, you're the first to get thrown into the fire. Hell, you're pretty much kindling.

Here's an unfortunate example: I had a pretty cushy, consistent job at the location that served as the mid-way point between "traditional school" and "Lil' Shawshank." The kid there *thought* they were absolute badasses...until they encountered the kids from Lil' Shawshank. Then they got shaken down, beaten up and quickly shown the error of their ways. Tanner was a kid that I had in my classes multiple times before; a super entitled, upper-middle-class white kids that *loved* throwing N-bombs into every other sentence. He was finishing his senior year at "Pre-Shawshank" because his previous school caught him with airline-sized bottles of liquor in his backpack, and Tanner would often refer to himself as a "dealer." He also had a history of making the girls in class uncomfortable by staring at them, licking his lips, and making inappropriate gestures.

Unsurprisingly, the other guys in class ate it up, and all of the attention and laughter bolstered his ego. The day I had him in my class for the 10th-ish time, the school had scheduled a fire drill, and notified the staff but not the students. As the alarm trilled, the kids hooted and hollered, heading out into the hall. The drill was over nearly as soon as it started, and the students all began trudging back to the room, grumbling. As Tanner passed me, he gave me an exaggerated wink, yelled "LEMME GET THAT TITTY!" and grabbed my nipple through my shirt and twisted. HARD.

I was in shock, and cycling through emotions: incredulity, annoyance, but most of all, *rage*. *"TANNER! OUTSIDE! NOW!"* My roar immediately silenced the room.

"Whassa matter? You got sensitive f*g titties or something?" Tanner smirked as he sauntered his way outside. A couple kids snickered, but the rest stared at me with eyes as big as hubcaps.

"We're going to the office" I growled, matter-of-factly and pointed him towards the admin building. Along the way, he fiddled with his phone nonchalantly. "It's cool--I'll just have my mom pick me up. I didn't want to stay the whole day anyway."

As we walked through the doors, Tanner strutted ahead and threw himself into the chair outside the vice principal's office, legs splayed out in front of him, phone in hand.

I walked into the VP's office, and he gestured lazily at the chairs in front of his desk. I declined the seat, and said "I'd like to report sexual battery and harassment." His eyes snapped up. Suddenly, I had his undivided attention. "You want to... *WHAT*?" I recounted the events to him, and his face reddened while he absently played with his tie and sputtered through excuses.

"You see, that's more...I mean...I'm sure he didn't *mean*...I mean. Well, let's...I...uh...let's get the SRO in here." And he darted out the door. Tanner caught some of what I said and was suddenly sitting at attention, back ramrod straight and *very* attentive to the VP.

The VP returned with the SRO following stiffly behind, and was immediately condescending to me. *"Heyyyyyyyyy bud. So I understand that there was a misunderstanding in class."* The SRO had that smug syrupy tone of a restaurant manager.

I was quick to correct him. "There's no misunderstanding: Tanner made a conscious decision to grab my nipple and twist it, while yelling, and I quote: 'let me get that titty.' He then asked if I had 'sensitive f*g titties' in front of the class. If I recall, that's considered hate speech at this school. I brought him down here immediately."

The VP coughed into his hand, stifling a smirk.

"Mmmmmm-HMMMMM." The SRO nodded, rubbing his hands together. "You see, there's not a clear-cut way to say that it was sexual though--he would need to grab your breast and hold on to it. Y'know, like almost fondling it and whatnot?"

"Let me be crystal clear," I hissed through clenched teeth. "He has a history of sexual harassment of female students and staff..."

"None that I have actual 'on-paper' reports of at this school, though" the VP quickly interjected.

"...And today was just another example of it. To say nothing of the hate speech."

"Well," the SRO gave me an exaggerated shrug "I mean *are* you gay though?"

I stared incredulously. The VP was quick to jump on my silence, and said "you know what? Why don't you take the rest of the afternoon off? It sounds like you've had a pretty rough morning." He smiled, and smoothed the paper on his desk. "How does that sound? Then we'll get to the bottom of this with Tanner. Rest assured, we take these kinds of things *very* seriously."

Before I could answer, he picked up the phone and called the secretary, instructing her to pay me the remaining hour and a half even though I was heading home early. I was furious, and disgusted, and more than anything, horribly disappointed in their response.

I declined the next three assignments at that site when they were offered to me.

I went from subbing at that school once a week to once a month. Then they removed me from the site pool completely. Mind you, I only found this out when I formally requested a copy of my file. The note from the principal's secretary requested that I not be assigned to that site, because "he uses a rude tone with administration and staff." The site never explained it to me, and the teachers that were requesting I cover their classes were baffled, because if they personally requested me as a sub, the secretary would tell them that I was booked on another assignment that day. I guess she didn't think that teachers and subs kept in touch outside of school.

Unfortunately, this wasn't the last time I experienced a bizarre "*about face*" from admin--but I eventually learned: they love you as long as you're getting shit done and not making waves. But the second you cast any manner of light on unfair practices, they'll find any reason to show you the door.

Another dose of awful was an experience I had subbing at a mod/severe site that I had never been placed at before. Now, let me tell you, the support team at that school was amazing: the ratio of paraprofessionals to students was 1:3, and for good reason. The kids were high school age, and all had pretty severe exceptional needs. I was coming in towards the end of the school year, and all the people on staff had built pretty great relationships with the kids, and were well aware of their schedules.

Tim, a linebacker-sized para, gave me the basic rundown. "So basically, all the kids here have routines: breakfast share-out, then exercise, snack, reading circle, lunch, recess, self-care, then games. Then your day's over. Pretty easy, right? Ok, so here's what you need to know about the kids in your room."

He went down the list. "Diana is prone to disrobing when she's frustrated, so just remind her that clothes stay on and she usually listens. Eric likes to keep his harness[15] on all day because it makes him feel safe. But watch out, because Jimmy likes to yank the back of the harness, and will even hook Eric on doorknobs if he's not paying attention." He continued down the roster and told me the do's and don'ts for all the kids in the class. "Your responsibility for the day is going to be Billy," he gestured to a kid sitting in the corner, absently poking at an iPad. Billy was barefoot, in denim overalls and a Green Day shirt, and had dirty blonde hair that jutted out from his head at odd angles. He looked over at me and gave me a thumbs up. Cool. We were already on the way to being buddies.

The school was like a giant, college-font letter O: the outside circle was the admin offices, conference rooms, staff lounges, and bathrooms. The classrooms were all facing the inner circle (more of a soft rectangle, really), and the very center of the O was a long-ish rec area with green grass, a little patch of flowers, some swings and a mini soccer field. Between the classrooms and the rec spot was a rubberized track, with a chest-high fence separating the track and the inner grassy area. At intervals, the fence had sliding gates, which would allow the teachers to close and lock off the rec access, essentially forcing the kids to walk the track if they left the classrooms...and that's exactly what they did.

The system was pretty ingenious--all of the classroom (and office) doors were locked from the outside, and if a kid had extra energy and jumped up to leave the classroom, they would exit into a giant, soft-floored circle where they could expend said energy without issue. There were also padded benches at odd intervals, so the kids walking the track could take periodic breaks. Also, if students were inside the O and another student tried to join them (and wasn't allowed to), the four-foot sliding gates would lock and deter them.

Billy's jam was that he would grab an old-school "twist and tick" kitchen timer once per hour and get "dirt time." When the para said that, I had kind of assumed that it was a colloquial way of saying "he gets to go outside and touch grass." Towards the end of the first hour, Billy's eyes were glued to the shelf with the various timers on them. At 10:54. He began to wiggle excitedly, and when 10:55 hit, he pointed emphatically, and grunted at me. "Sure bud, go ahead."

In a flash he was out of his chair, across the room and out the door, timer in hand. I followed him outside to the grassy area, and he made a beeline to the small flower garden that the kids all maintained. Without warning, he dug his toes into the dirt and began sifting through the soil, giggling excitedly the whole time. He would plop down and crabwalk around the dirt, kick piles over and rake his toes through the upturned dirt. This was the purest, most unfettered display of joy I had ever seen, and before I knew it, the jarring *BZZZIIIIIIINGG* of the timer broke the moment. I said "Ok bud, time to head back in!" Billy's shoulders sank, and he started to get up...and then sat down in a huff. "C'mon bud, that was your five minutes. We need to head in and get cleaned up before lunch, ok?"

Billy tossed his head at me, snorted derisively, and crossed his arms across his chest.

One of the other classroom teachers, Jennie, called over to him. "Hey Billy? We need to head in now, m'kay?" He snapped his head in her direction, grunted, and made a "go away" motion with his hands. "Ohhh come on now," she sang back to him, "you don't want to lose your dirt time this afternoon, do you?"

Billy's eyes shot open comically, and he stood up quickly, heading towards her. Jennie had already made her way into the center area with us, but then she froze. "How good are you at flag football?" she asked, voice strained.

"Why?"

Before she could answer me, Billy charged her. I watched Jennie juke deftly, spinning just out of his reach. Almost in unison, the other three teachers ran out of their rooms and slammed the sliding gates facing their rooms shut, locking Billy, Jennie, and me in the center area.

Oh boy.

Billy howled, and ran at me, fists clenched, and I waited until he was almost on me, then clumsily mimicked Jennie's spin. Billy shot past me, and ran into the grassy area. He charged her again, with the same result. After repeating this two or three more times, he sank to his knees in the grass, and rocked.

Self-stimulating (aka "stimming") behavior is a way that many non-verbal kids help regulate their emotions, so I let myself relax a little. "He just...doesn't like...losing...his...free time" Jennie panted as she approached me. With minimal success, I was trying to mask my own panting with deep breaths. I stood between Jennie and Billy, hoping to mitigate another attempted tackle. Billy was still rocking himself and seemed to have lost all interest in us. "So how often...does this...happen?"

Jennie shrugged. "Once or twice a week. We just run it out of him whenever possible. The easiest way to wear him out is to run." She paused. "Run! *RUN!*" Her eyes were huge as she yelled the last two words, and I realized *wayyyy* too late that I had fully turned my back on Billy.

I spun around just fast enough to see his fist descending towards my face, as if in slow motion. His punch bounced off my deaf ear, literally and figuratively ringing my bell, as my hearing aid screeched, then went silent.

I was dazed, but I noticed his shock at the loud electronic squeal, and he looked scared. He turned and bolted back towards the flowers and dirt, where he sank down and rocked himself again. Two of the other paras waved me over to an open gate, and got us out of the center and away from him.

"Hey man, you're bleeding," one of them chirped. "Staff bathroom's over there." I clumsily unlocked the bathroom, to find that my ear was bleeding and that my hearing aid had broken off *inside* my ear. Stupidly, I dug out the two pieces as a high, sustained whine of tinnitus began in my head.

Awesome.

I checked in with the front desk, wrote up an injury report and headed into urgent care. After a quick check-up, the doc concluded that the bleeding was from a scrape from the broken plastic of the hearing aid, and sent me home with a smear of antibiotic ointment on the inner edge of my ear.

The next morning, I called the school to inquire about my hearing aid. The site was completely sympathetic, and Jennie (along with two other paras) wrote down their account of what happened, corroborating my story. They suggested I file an insurance claim to the district immediately, and referred me to Rick Majors, the HR person that handles site insurance.

Rick, a dead ringer for Guy Smiley, called me two days later. "So I hear you had an *unfortunate* accident in a classroom a couple days ago."

"You mean getting attacked in the quad by a student with a history of violent, physical responses and getting my hearing aid broken *inside* my head?"

"Yes, *thaaat*." His voice dripped with cloyingly fake sympathy. "What was it you were hoping we could do for you?"

"Um, for starters, you could replace my hearing aid. And my ear has swollen up pretty bad."

"Look...uh...MacArthur? Can I call you Mac? *Mac*, we understand that you already went to urgent care after you filed your claim at the school. Did they not treat you?"

"They gave me antibiotics for the cut..."

"...So they *did* render aid?"

"Yes, but..."

"...Well, let's table the ear for now. You're expecting us to replace your...uh...earphone?"

"No. Not headphone. My *HEARING* AID."

"Right. *That.* Well, unfortunately, we cannot be held responsible for the personal electronic devices you bring into such a...*volatile* environment. Look, we have subs get their phones and iPads broken all the time. It's considered an assumed risk at these sites."

"I *know* you didn't just equate my hearing aid with an iPad..."

"Unfortunately, the district will. And like the amount for *other* personal electronics, we are prepared to offer you $250 towards replacing it."

I was aghast. "Are you aware of how much hearing aids cost?"

He snickered on the other end of the line. "I am...but that's, unfortunately, the best we can do. Do you have homeowners' insurance?"

"*WHAT?*"

"Because you can file a claim for your homeowners' insurance and that can go towards the deductible."

"No. I'm not going to file through my..."

"Mac? I have another call coming in, I'll need to call you back. Ok? Bye." The phone clicked off.

I was fuming. Who in the *actual fuck* did this guy think...

My phone buzzed again, this time from an UNKNOWN CALLER.

"Hey Mac. It's Rick. I need to make this quick, because I'm calling from my cell. Look, I'm gonna level with you: you probably aren't going to get jack from this hearing aid thing. Literally the *best* I can do is offer you $500 flat towards your deductible. I'm going to call you back, and offer the $250. Then I'll make a big deal of saying I'll call *my* boss, then I'll call back with a $500 offer. And buddy, I'd take it. If you decline the $500 offer, you'll need to take us to small claims court, and the district will *absolutely* keep you tied up in paperwork for at *least* another six months. If you need to get it quick--*and it sounds like you do*--I would take the $500. If you don't, there's no guarantee that it will *ever* get replaced. I'm gonna call you back in five minutes, ok?" He disconnected again.

I was floored. What kind of fucking organization would fight an insurance claim that happened on their *own* property. And with witnesses!? My inner weasel smugly replied *The kind of organization that has things like this happen on their property all the time.*

The phone rang again. *"Heya Mac? Rick Majors here.* Have you thought any more about that $250 towards your deductible?"

"Yeah Rick. $250 isn't enough. My deductible is higher."

"Gotcha. Let me call my boss and see what other numbers I can come up with..."

We went through his fake hemming and hawing, and eventually, he offered me the $500. He was too slick and matter-of-fact about it, and even though he was a scumbag, I completely believed that the district would fight me in court about it. There's that whole thing about preferring getting stabbed in the front to getting stabbed in the back, I guess? In the end, I was able to get the hearing aid replaced with the $500 and my insurance deductible. But unfortunately for me, it wasn't the last scumbag admin I ever had to deal with.

Yet another great example of staff frustration happened when I was subbing for a 12th-grade English class. Most of the day had gone swimmingly, and we were settling into the post-lunch humdrum, where most kids (and adults) struggled to keep themselves awake. It was nearly summer, and the pressing heat and Senioritis weren't helping to keep the kids engaged. Of all the classes I had covered that day, the "after lunch squad" were clearly the most studious ones. They sat down immediately and took out their work and a couple even asked if they could put in their earbuds to work more efficiently.

The class was so positive and well-behaved that I was having trouble staying awake myself. Instead of dozing, I resorted to walking laps around the room, weaving between the rickety "all in one" metal and graphite desks that all seemed to have a permanent wobble. I made my way to the front of the room, and leaned on the lectern.

The door slammed open and MegaChad burst into the room in full bro-mode. To paint a picture, he was probably 5'5, medium length blonde curly hair, sunglasses, tank top and board shorts.

"WHAT'S UP FUCKERS?! I HEARD MALONEY WAS OUT TODAY!"

The group seemed to murmur a collective moan, and I could practically hear their eyes rolling inside their skulls.

I moved on him. "Hey man, I respect the energy but this group was…"

"I rEsPeCt YoUr EnErGy…" he parroted back in a "hurr durr" voice. Nobody laughed. He grinned and said "look man, I'm just trying to *shake up* the room!" He went down one aisle, shoving books and papers off desks and to the floor. When he got to the desk of Larry, a student with obvious physical disabilities, I had closed the distance to him.

"Ok man, time to go. If you don't, I'll call security and have…"

"And tell them what? I'm just *SHAKIN' IT UP, BRO!*" As he said that, he tried to lift Larry and the desk up together, which sent Larry tumbling to the floor. I quickly helped him to his feet; he seemed dazed but ok. I turned and clapped my hands on MegaChad's shoulders, physically moving him towards the door.

"Dude, *don't fuckin' touch me!* My dad's gonna be…"

"I DON'T CARE WHO YOUR FATHER IS! GET OUT OF MY ROOM NOW!" My roar flooded the uncharacteristically quiet room and every eye was on me. MegaChad turned and squared his shoulders at me.

"Touch me one more time and I'll…"

"YOU'LL *WHAT!*?"

Mind you, this was early in my career before I had learned better de-escalation strategies…but he had just assaulted a disabled student, and I was livid.

MegaChad stepped towards me, fists up but shoulders slumped. "I'LL KNOCK YOU THE FUCK OUT, BRO!"

Knowing that I couldn't actually fight a 18-year old kid (no matter how much I wanted to), I took a mental step back.

I grinned at him. "What's your best case scenario? You knock me out? If I topple over on you, I'll crush your noodle-armed body under my significantly larger self. Or you swing and whiff, and get arrested for assaulting a teacher. Either way. I'm here for it. So time to decide."

MegaChad legitimately thought about it, and in an uncharacteristic moment of pure realization, he yelled "*Maaaaan, FUCK you!*" and threw himself out of the classroom.

I followed him and yelled "go STRAIGHT to the VP! I'm calling security now!"

I punched in the security extension and it rang for more than a minute, and nobody picked up. I tried calling two more times, with no success.

"Chad's just gonna ditch," a girl said. "I need to go to the bathroom anyway. Want me to stop by the office and tell them his name?"

"Sure!" I dialed the number again. Still no reply. Great.

After the girl left, I checked again on Larry. He seemed nervous but ok. "I'm sorry I fell, mister."

"You have *nothing* to apologize for, bud. That kid was awful."

He shrugged. "I could have given him my seat. I think he wanted it."

Before I could reply, the door banged open again, and I turned, ready for the worst.

Instead, a tiny bald-headed school security officer rushed into the room, eyes blazing.

I waved to him. "The guy you're looking for just…"

"JUST WHO DO YOU THINK YOU ARE!?"

"Wait…*What?*"

"WHO THE HELL DO YOU THINK YOU ARE!?"

"Mac Shaw, charmed." I stuck out my hand. "Now, look. A kid just…"

"YOU THINK YOU'RE SO GODDAMN SMART!? YOU *REALLY* SENT A GIRL TO WALK A STUDENT TO THE OFFICE?" The diminutive guy was purple, literally spitting foam towards me with every word.

"That's not what actually…"

"…BECAUSE THAT'S EXACTLY WHAT YOU DID!"

"Ok, I think you should step outside and calm down, little fella."[16]

"I should *WHAAAAAT*!?" His eyes shot open even wider.

"Yeah, if you're going to stand there and scream and cuss in front of the classroom, as a school security officer, you're not setting the best example. So yeah. Please step outside and compose yourself."

From behind me, Larry plaintively said "I fell down but I'm ok. I think he wanted my seat."

I watched the security guard look from the kid to me, seeming to fight an internal battle. He ended up yelling what could only be described as "FFFFFFPPPPPPPPPPPP!" before leaving in a huff.

Unsurprisingly, at the end of the day, my shiny-domed friend was waiting in the office for me, still visibly agitated.

The VP rubbed his hands together as I turned in my keys. "Mr. Shaw, we would like to meet with you in…"

"So I just stayed an extra 20 minutes helping out a kid, which puts me after school hours. Will this be a paid meeting?"

Before the VP could reply, the security guard jumped in and sputtered "…are you? *ARE YOU KIDDING!? No!*"

"Then I'm afraid I must decline. I'm happy to document what happened, but I'm not a fan of having a kid who wasn't even in my class physically assault one of my students with disabilities. I'm not sure who the kid was that came in, but I'm sure the students in the class can identify him for you. He also threatened to punch me, after going around the room and pushing multiple students' work on the floor. After it happened, I called the security office four times without an answer. He couldn't be bothered to pick up the phone, but was quick to show up in my room and cuss me out, though. The young lady that stopped into the office offered to do so on her way to the bathroom, on account of that particular student having a history of ditching class. I know your little buddy is eager to yell at me again, but I'd suggest you have him get his own house in order before criticizing anyone else's."

I watched the little bald guy go purple again, sputtering furious consonants. I had to look away, because he was starting to resemble a purple penis in a blue uniform.

The VP smiled thinly and said "Well, I was told a different set of events. I think you will be removed from tomorrow's assignment in that room."

"Suit yourself, I'm easy."

Sure enough, on my way home, my phone rang announcing that I was taken off the assignment. I called Maloney (who I'd covered for dozens of times before) to tell him about what happened.

"Jesus man, I'm sorry. Chad does shit like that all the time. Don't sweat it. I'm sure everything'll come out in the wash."

"Yeah I kinda doubt it. The little security guard was pretty angry."

"I wouldn't sweat it."

Sure enough, three days later I get a call from the VP. Turns out that NINE students wrote accounts of what happened unprompted, and left them at the main office. MegaChad actually got expelled two days later for bringing a knife on campus and threatening another student.

"I just wanted to pass along my apologies for not contacting you sooner. It's just that...you know...it's just...yeah."

"'*It's just that you know it's just yeah?*' No, No I don't know what that means. Please elaborate."

Even over the phone, I could hear the VP squirming. "It's just that we had to react quickly is all."

"Sure. Only now I don't feel super comfortable working at your site. So if it's all the same, I think I'll continue working elsewhere.

"Well that's *your* choice." I could hear the VP frowning through the phone.

"Indeed it is. Have the day that you deserve."

"...WHAT?!"

I hung up on him.

You see, a *lot* of admin (just like a lot of human beings) are incredibly petty. Even if I had come back to that site, they would jump at the first chance to blacklist me again, if only to prove themselves right. So in a lot of ways, I had dodged yet another bullet.

The absolute worst example of admin leadership happened when I was doing a long-term subbing gig at a high school in a middle- to upper-class district (with a decidedly non-diverse student body). The class was "Intro to Coding" and it was almost all mega-privileged, 11th graders (with a smattering of 12th graders scrambling to pick up another elective or risk summer school). Most had better personal laptops, and chose not to use the lab's school-provided desktop PCs.

I had won them over by the third day by bringing in snacks (*"thanks again for coming to my 'bribe kids with snacks' Ted Talk"*), and thought I had the class pretty much pinned down; I knew a bit about coding and was helping them with their end of the year projects: designing a basic webpage. Easy.

The computer lab was set up similar to many you've probably seen: five rows of tables, all facing the front of the room, with an aisle down the middle and the teacher's desk whiteboard/screen at the front. I'd project the day's assignment on the pull-down screen and keep it on throughout the class.

On Friday of that week, I was making my usual classroom rounds, chatting and checking in on their work, when I noticed the two kids in the front-most row of the room: the guy had his head lolled back and was grinning as he stared, glassy-eyed, up at the ceiling. The kids sitting directly behind him were cracking up and recording him on their phones. I figured he was high (as many of the kids often were at this school) and moved to check in on him. Then I noticed that his hoodie was in his lap... And the girl next to him was bouncing her hand under it.

"ARE YOU... REALLY?!" I didn't mean to bark out the question as loud as I did; I just sort of yelled words, incredulous, as the girl slowly withdrew her hand...and went back to typing, never even looking in my direction.

"NO...JUST...GOD! DON'T TOUCH THE KEYBOARD...GET UP! JUST GO WASH YOUR HANDS! GOOD LORD... GO. WASH. YOUR. HANDS. RIGHT. NOW!"

She stood up and bolted from the room, face bright red.

The boy just smirked at me. "What's *your* problem?"

I strode to the front of the room, furious, and called security, struggling with the best way to say "hand job" over the phone.

Security came and grabbed the kid, and brought him to the office. Later, after I dismissed the class (and wiped down the door handles and surfaces with bleach wipes), the office called my room and requested that I stop in before I left. I had the room keys, so I had to anyway.

The VP brought me into the office with another admin, and told me that the student said that I just started yelling at him, and that the girl was just grabbing her phone from out of his pocket.

"If she was really getting her phone, then she was taking her time, and must have dropped it up and down several dozen times."

The VP rolled his eyes. "Well, did you take *video* of the incident?"

I was stunned. "Let me get this straight: I catch a kid getting a hand job during class--*allegedly*--and your first question to me is 'did I record it?!' No. I'm sorry. I didn't think to record teenagers engaging in sexual acts on my phone. I'm not in a huge rush to be on the nightly news, if it's all the same to you."

The VP's face turned scarlet, as he struggled to come up with a retort. The other admin was suddenly very interested in his phone.

After he stammered something about "lack of proof and unprofessional language" he dismissed me for the day.

Later that night, I got an email that I was removed from the assignment.

I called the next morning for clarification, and the VP wouldn't take my call. I called three more times and sent two emails, CCing the classroom teacher as well.

He eventually called back a week later, and told me that he

wanted to apologize, and that the same students were *'caught in another compromising situation'*, and 'would I like to come back and teach that class again.'

I took a deep breath. "With *no* due respect, sir: please go kick rocks in flip flops."

"Excuse me?"

"I said *KICK. ROCKS. IN. FLIP. FLOPS.*"

Listening to him gargle with rage on the other end of the phone was glorious, and when he hung up, I knew I was blacklisted from yet another site. Didn't care. Worth it.

Chapter 14:

"In Praise Of 'Difficult' Parents"

The world of substitute teaching is, hopefully, in my rearview and now that I'm a "real" teacher (as my kids *loooove* to remind me) I have more parent meetings each year than I'd care to count.[17] I can't tell you the sheer number of parents that come into these meetings with guns drawn and hammers pulled back. I get it--there are parents who have been on the receiving end of shit-tier teachers for years and are very much of the mind that nobody is fighting for their kid...so they *need* to.

When I first started out teaching and was observing parent meetings, I was shocked how many meetings would end with someone leaving the room in tears. I would see teachers freeze up and I'd watch parents seethe, building up their anger until they crashed over the teachers like a wave on a rock. Nine times out of ten, it would be about a misunderstanding or miscommunication, and instead of pushing the reset button and asking for a quick pause, the teacher would backpedal...and the parent pounced.

Oddly enough, when I encountered a parent like this for the first time, I used the same strategy that I used on their kid: "I'm sensing that you might be frustrated about something. Can we name it, write it down, and make a conscious effort to address it?" Just like that: instant deflation. I wasn't using excuses or nebulous language or looking to my admin for a bailout; I was flat-out saying "something's fucky, and I want to make sure we get it handled." I've found that by listening to their concerns without waiting to give an immediate response, and writing down notes about what they say, they're far less inclined to anger. Plus, when they see you actually *writing their words down* they tend to be more careful about their word choices.

Setting ground rules to parent meetings is another way to assert and maintain control without seeming like you're doing so. I usually draft up an agenda for the meeting, and if the parent starts bringing up extraneous shit, I can decide whether or not to add it to the day's agenda, or to add it at the bottom for a future meeting. Similarly, if you have parents that are prone to outbursts, you can redirect them to the agenda items. If they continue, take a 3 minute break and leave the room. Go get a drink of water (or Jameson) and get your shit together.

Also worth mentioning, if you know that the parent has a history of going off the handle, be sure to invite your admin or a third party as an observer. Barring that, inform them that you will be recording the meeting, *"in order to make sure the notes you take are as complete as possible."*

Even when saying all of this, I can legitimately count on one hand the amount of times that a parent has continued to be aggressive after we effectively communicated to them that we're *all* on the same side, and genuinely have their child's best interest at heart. And for bonus points, refer to examples of their work, or things that they did that shows growth. When they push for something outrageous, be strict but fair, and explain to them why it's not going to happen in neutral terms...just don't tell them a flat "no."

Lastly, as I alluded to earlier: all that vitriol comes from somewhere, so try to get to the root of their problem. Most difficult parents just feel like they aren't being heard, so just reframe their issue with something like "so if I'm understanding you correctly, you're frustrated with (*insert topic here*). That makes sense to me. Let's look at our options." It's hard for them to stay pissed when you're showing them that you hear their concerns, and want to work together to fix them. Even if you *don't* want to help them, just making them feel heard is half the battle.

If there's one thing I can offer to new teachers (and reinforce to parents) it's this: always stick to your goddamn boundaries-- and I needed to remind myself of that more often than I'd care to admit, especially during the first couple years when I'd be grading papers and answering emails from parents past midnight.

My phenomenal therapist once told me about a client of hers that was a pediatrician and had difficulty leaving work at the office. He had challenges overthinking things from the day, and was stressing out and losing sleep. They came up with a system where the act of taking off his stethoscope and hanging it above his desk meant he was done being a doctor for the day.

I took a page from this doctor's plan, and I have a pair of "teaching shoes" that I wear solely on days where I'm teaching, and as long as those shoes are on my feet, I'm in "teacher mode."

It definitely helps me differentiate between work and home time, and it makes ignoring calls/emails feel less shitty.

Now, if I can ask you parents to do one thing for us, it would be to not call or email us with non-emergencies.

I can't tell you how many times I get a phone or email chirp asking me what their child's PowerSchool or ClassDojo password is, when holiday break starts or what day the school play is on. So many of these questions can be answered by checking the school page or searching your email account. Yet, whenever I see an email from a parent sent after 6 p.m., morbid curiosity gets the best of me, and I open it; and in nearly eleven years, I can count on one hand the number of times it's ended up being something good.

Boundaries are equally important inside your classroom as outside it. I've run classrooms where students called teachers and staff by their first names, and others where they stiffly refer to you as "Mister," "Miss," "Sir" and "Ma'am." I remember the early days of Lil' Shawshank, where teachers had literal lines drawn out on the floor around their desks in red duct tape that students weren't allowed to cross.

Conversely, I've had rooms with a fully stocked snack pantry, and students were allowed to help themselves to food entirely on the honor system. The most interesting part was that these hippie commune classrooms would often be in the same building as the micromanager *uber-alles* classrooms, and kids being placed in one room or another was literally the luck of the draw. Unsurprisingly, many of the "strict room" students would elect to take their lunches with their friends in the "hippie room."

One boundary I tend to be pretty lax on is the *"my lunchtime is my time"* boundary. Once you start building positive relationships with students, you'll find that they might feel safer in your classroom than others, and more often than not, great teachers will find their classrooms to be hangout spots during lunchtime and free periods. This wasn't always the case, as you'll see later on.

The biggest part of maintaining boundaries is managing expectations--if you're polite but firm about your expectations from day one, and actively reinforce and remind students of them when they're approaching the line, I promise that you'll end up with positive results more often than not.

For example, one of the greatest ideas I ever poached was co-creating a "Day 1 Class Expectations" list with the students and sticking with it all year. I mean, we've all been in a class where teachers bark out a set of orders like "no talking when I'm talking!" and "RAISE YOUR HAND IF YOU HAVE SOMETHING TO SAY!" I've also been in classes where open dialogue is encouraged, and kids learn to step into the natural ebb and flow of academic conversations.

Co-creating class expectations with your students is a killer way to achieve this, in a way that makes students feel like they're being heard, while building a sense of belongingness and classroom ownership at the same time. For example, instead of saying *"these are the rules that I expect you to follow every day,"* you can ask them pointed questions like "What makes a good classroom? What are some rules that we can all stick by each day?" Sure, you'll get some wacky things like *"every day at 2 p.m., we howl at the clock"*...but you'll also hear kids begin to self-regulate, and say some of the things that they expect, like "be in your seat and ready to learn by 8:05." Then, when kids are getting out of pocket, you can point to the rules that *they* made and remind themm of learning expectations.

Now that I have my own classroom, I genuinely look forward to doing this at the start of each school year, just to see what crazy shit each new group of kids comes up with.

One of the best classrooms I ever worked in had "**always respect the boogie box**" written at the bottom of their class rules, almost as an afterthought. I asked one of the kids what the boogie box was, and she solemnly pointed at the ragged 3'x3' masking tape square on the floor near the door. She giggled as I furrowed my eyebrows in confusion.

"If you accidentally walk through the boogie box, you have to stop and dance for at least five seconds, and it doesn't matter if there's music or not. You still have to dance."

"What happens if you don't dance, though?"

"Oh you *definitely* want to dance."

"And if I don't?"

"You go outside, and we all get to pelt you with rotten lutefisk[18], and yell 'shame!'"

I raised an eyebrow.

"See? You should probably just dance."

"How often has this happened?"

"Never. 'Cause everyone *always* dances." She grinned at me. "You

182

can be the first, if you want?"

May 19th, 2014:

"Where is your God now?!"

This month, I happen to teach six classes, with one period for prep.

For those who are unaware, most teachers have one or two periods designated as "prep." This empty, student less period is designed to give you a little extra time to prepare for the rest of your other classes.

Most teachers use this time to make copies, grade papers and tests, run errands or, in many cases, go out to their car, where they can let off long primal screams into a pillow that may or may not end with them passing out.

This is also known as "teacher nap time." It keeps us level, and allows us to clear our mental cache…which in turn, allows your children to live another day.

In the school I'm currently working at, even though you're technically on prep, you're supposed to make yourself available if students want to meet, do make up work or receive extra tutoring. No biggie, since I tend to run pre and post school study sessions, and students rarely want to sacrifice a study hall spent taking selfies, to actually do schoolwork.

Unfortunately, there's a student that would seek out my room every prep period to visit. At first, he said he needed extra help with the Rome chapter we were working on. No biggie. But after the third visit, I realized he just wanted to come into the room, and parrot whatever we talked about in class, or whatever he read (or saw on TV), in an effort to show me how smart he was.

Look, I get precocious kids; I was one. But a student who won't leave after I shower him with praise? There comes a breaking point where I simply have no more congratulations, and I can't muster the faintest bit of positivity.

He's a praise vampire, and though I know he gets a ton of support and recognition at home, he always wants more.

This particular student, though incredibly bright and clever, is one of the most OCD students I've ever met. He'll walk through the room before and after class to make sure that pens aren't left on the floor. He'll reposition the erasers on the board, re sort homework piles and straighten stacks of tests after he turns his in.

Usually this works to my benefit, as I get an unofficial TA to help out with basic classroom tasks; but when I'm on prep, he zeroes in on my room and won't stop until he gets in. He's like a demonic Sheldon Cooper, obsessively knocking at Penny's door.

And here's the thing: even though we're on prep, I'm still supposed to answer the door, and help the student in whatever way possible…even if they aren't really looking for extra help.

After weeks of spending the majority of my free

period sitting with our little chatterbox, a thought occurred to me: what if I do something so incredibly simple, that I could get him to avoid my room like the plague?

So three days ago, I started putting an image on the projector during my prep. It showed 20 immaculately sharpened pencils in a row, with one towards the middle reversed, pointing upward and slightly at an angle.

The first day, he came in, stared at the image and asked me to "fix it, or turn it off." I told him that I couldn't, since it was for the next class. The next day, he came in, looked at it, yelled "NOPE!" and left. The third day he just looked from the hallway and shook his head. And I got to enjoy a blissful lunch.

The kid never bothered me again after that day. Evil? Maybe. But he learned.

Chapter 15:

"Murder Mediocrity And Get Shit Done"

I haven't minced words before, so why start now? **There are a *lot* of shit teachers out there.** And believe me when I say that I'll be the first to throw myself on the sword when the time comes. The previous chapters have shown plenty of things I'm ashamed of...but I *always* learned from them. I've had the honor of working alongside some of the most incredible people to ever pick up a dry-erase marker, and I'm continually humbled in their presence.

But.
For every stellar teacher, there are 10 or more mediocre dawdlers, content to mosey through a career, blindly and blissfully unaware of the chaos they leave in their wake.

Case in point: let's look at Tim Dobbs, a veteran teacher at Lil' Shawshank. Tim was a particular favorite of the students, because he had several TV's set up around his classroom with

Xboxes attached to them. I'm no stranger to gaming, so my first instinct (like many of the students) was to absolutely deify him.

I realized weeks later, that the kids were spending 70+% of their class time playing Xbox instead of learning about the content. And this was a history and world cultures class, so I was *pretty* sure that the kids had a lot to pick up.

Every day that I subbed in that class was exactly the same: students would filter in, pick up the two packets, and sit down to work. I never really spent a lot of time looking over their work, because we aren't paid to grade assignments. However, after the third week, Mitty (one of the kiddos with processing challenges) asked me for help with an answer.

"I know all the answers are here," he gestured at the second packet "but it just doesn't make a whole lot of sense." I took a closer look at his work. The two packet system was relatively simple: students would pick up the first packet, and write their name across the top. They'd pick up the second packet, and read that to figure out the answers to put into the first packet. At the end of class, they would turn in packet one to me, and return packet two to the table at the front of the classroom for the next group of kids to use.

Mitty handed me packet two, and as I looked over the second packet, I froze. The second packet literally had *all* of the answers numbered and underlined. No, that couldn't *possibly* be right. Maybe a kid just answered on the wrong page. So I looked at the stack of Packet #2's for the next class--the answers were printed on the pages, and the numbers and underlines were actually handwritten--so I couldn't say "oh, maybe he just printed the answer key by mistake."

Mitty's issue was that one of the questions had multiple answers, and he was confused why only one was underlined. I suggested that he handwrite in the other answer in the space below the line.

Before I left for the day, I wrote down Mitty's "question" in Dobbs' sub notes. When I came in the next week, there was a brand new set of packets...also with their answers numbered and underlined. I realized why kids loved his class *so* damn much--there was zero rigor, and he was quite literally giving kids all the answers. And his class was considered a double period, so as long as the kids copied their work down quickly, they could have up to 90 minutes of free time to play *Halo*, *FIFA* or *Madden*. And if he was ever audited, he'd have a portfolio of work that backed up all the straight A's that nearly every student had. The second packets would mysteriously vanish, of course.

I was dumbstruck. I mean I *get* it: many of the teachers at Lil' Shawshank were well aware of the challenges that our students faced, and would flub an assessment or two to help the kids boost their grade. But this was ridiculous.

That day I learned an important lesson: it's not the bad teachers that we need to worry about...it's the indifference of tenured teachers who are content to coast through their later years.

I can't tell you how many times I'd sub for a class, and the teacher's directions were "play the DVD in the player for the class, and tell each student to write down five things they noticed." I legitimately think that was part of the *Mediocre Teacher Handbook*, because I encountered this set of directions in 25+ classrooms 11 years subbing.

The absolute worst example of this was a 50-minute art class that I covered early in my sub career, where the only instructions were "start the movie and have them watch until the bell rings." Considering that the first 15 minutes consisted of getting kids settled and taking attendance, that only left 35ish minutes for the movie. Easy peasy, lemon squeezy...right?

You know what fucking movie she chose to show for *six fucking periods*? Pixar's *"Up."*

If you haven't yet seen that masterpiece, consider this a spoiler alert: the first 30ish minutes set up a lovely romance between Carl and Ellie, a couple of middle-aged adventure-seekers. Pixar does a beautiful job of illustrating the courtship, romance and beautiful marriage of the childless couple, and ultimately shows them growing old, with Ellie eventually succumbing to an aggressive cancer, leaving Carl alone and lost, in the house they built together.

All of that happens in the first 30ish minutes...and I got to watch it *six times in one fucking day*; each viewing digging me a little deeper into the depression hole.

In almost every "show the video and write down five things" instance, there was never a chance to debrief the movie with students or even explore the concepts they viewed. It was busy work: a placating, lazy lesson plan that was, quite frankly, an insult to the art students.

And "read this packet and answer the multiple choice questions" isn't any better. The kids aren't toddlers--they know when you're assigning busy work in lieu of actual content.

I would have kids tell me things like "I like when you're here, because you talk to us like people...and you don't come in smelling *weird*.[19] And you actually answer our questions truthfully.

I honestly don't get it: if you hate your job (or worse, feel *nothing* about it), why not quit? Find something you're passionate about and take a run at it. Life's amazing, and *far* too fucking short to toil away in a job you hate. As someone who's worked literally dozens of jobs, from gas station attendant to IT specialist, there are *plenty* of options out there. Don't ever feel like you're tied to an "at will" job.

Look, I get it: it's easy to find yourself complacent in a system, and doing the minimum to get a "good enough" paycheck is fine. But is that what you really want out of life? If the movie you're watching is shit, why sit through it to the credits? There are plenty of other offerings in the multiplex, and there's bound to be one that excites you and makes you *want* to be there.

My extra-severe grandmother once told me "even if you end up being a ditch-digger, you should work your hardest to be the *best* ditch-digger ever!" And listen, if the previous chapters have told you anything, my career as a teacher has been a 12-year exercise in continual refinement, bracketed by *magnificent* fuckery. I'm barely above awful, but I keep working at it, because I want to be the best damn teacher I can be. If you're in a job where you've given up, why not leave and give someone else a try?

Too many "teachers" are just mediocre workers who plugged themselves into a career, but give zero fucks about their responsibility, and are seemingly only in it for the paycheck. And those jobs are *fine*...just not when you're responsible for shaping young minds. Trust me, there are *plenty* of jobs out there that require a bare minimum of responsibility succeed--and I've worked at least 12 of 'em.

One of the best things you can do to stop the shit cycle is to check in with peers you trust, and have them audit your class. Do lesson-tuning protocols when you're stagnating; sure they come across as hokey at first, but I guarantee you'll get something out of the process. And just because something worked five years ago doesn't mean it's still relevant now.

I cannot stress this enough: check in with your kids...especially if you teach high school. I remember a journalism professor who was adamant that we all needed to know how to typeset text on a massive printing press, in the event of the collapse of modern society, and spent two weeks walking us through the process. Mind you, this was a 300-level class, and we burned valuable time that could have been better spent learning to self-edit and write compelling content (as you've no doubt noticed). By getting lesson input from students, you learn to adapt your teaching to encompass different learning profiles and get an idea of what your students actually *need.*

And for fuck's sake, English teachers listen up: stop defaulting to Romeo and Juliet when the curriculum requires Shakespeare. If you aren't pointing out how, on page one, the Capulets literally start bragging about how they're going to rape and murder Montague women randomly--because *everyone* in the play (save for Juliet and Benvolio) is a piece of shit--and how the *entire* play is a roast on the concept of teenage love, then why even bother teaching it at all?[20] If you're going to study Shakespeare, start by showing them the video of a compelling performance and explain concepts...*then* get into the dry-ass reading.

Another thought worth mentioning: if you don't give a shit about what you're teaching, then why would your kids give a shit (I mean, aside from chasing that brass ring of "good grades")?

I can tell you, in my four years of teaching *actual* classes and eleven-ish years of long-term subbing, if you can't provide a tangible example of practical application of what you're teaching, you're bound to lose 40+ percent of your class. Sure, they'll go through the rote bullshit to get a passing grade, but if your goal is to get any degree of buy-in, you need to take a long, hard look at the *why.* And if you're going to assign a brand new lab or a project, you should run through it a couple of times through different lenses; will an English learner have challenges that a native speaker might? How about a student with processing disabilities? And so on.

As someone who spent several years in the food service and retail industry, I can unequivocally state that we as a society would be far better people if a year of service work was compulsory. We'd treat store workers and restaurant staff better, and minimize the class divide that comes with working a "professional" job instead of a blue-collar one. Similarly, I have found that the greatest administrators and higher-ups are teachers who have ascended to the next level of the layer cake...but haven't forgotten where they came from. Likewise, it should go without saying, but some of the greatest single-subject teachers have a background in special education, which means they can differentiate instruction far more readily than teachers without that training.

And speaking of special education, can we cut the shit with this one-size-fits-all approach to classrooms? We love to extoll the virtues of the mighty LRE[21], but rarely want to step outside our comfort zone and *truly* differentiate instruction. More often than not, this results in the lessons being tailored to the lowest ability level in class, with the rest of the kids expected just to follow along.

I'm fully aware how incredibly challenging this is, and if we're truly going to put the "individual" in "individual education plan," it's going to take quite a lot of work. So start by tapping your special education teachers (or reach out to your general ed teachers if you're an Education Specialist) and start the ball rolling.

I'm a bit of a bleeding heart, but I'm a firm believer that the lift doesn't have to be awful, especially if you have enough people helping you.

October 12th, 2015:

"Syrup means never having to say you're sorrey."

Teaching high school "kids" is a challenge, mostly because they're supposed to come to me as nearly finished cookies, with the last bit of baking done, so as not to send them into the world as "soft on the inside, barely baked snickerdoodles."

No, I strive to have them leave my classroom as firm, brick like biscotti that will chip the tooth of the jackass that's foolish enough to try to take a big bite out of them.

At least that's how I see it.

Anyway, I've noticed a LOT of this uninspired "oh, sorry" or "mahh bad" shit as of late.

Caught you taking duck face selfies? "Oh shit; sorry, Mr. Shaw."

You got caught calling the quiet girl a "weird, dumb bitch?" "Sorry, Mr. Shaw."

Trying (and failing) to cheat off a friend's test? "Mah bad! I'm sorry, Mr. Shaw."

Late for class (AKA our time)? "Oh, uh…I'm sorry, Shaw."

So I decided to institute something new in my classroom.

After hearing too many "I'm sorry's" this semester (AND IT'S ONLY OCTOBER!), I told my kids there's a difference between "sorry" and "sorrey."

"Sorry" is a cheap, easy out for kids who are just concerned that they got caught; "sorrey" is a sincere Canadian apology that not only shows pure contrition as the student seeking forgiveness KNOWS that they're caught (no shit) but also, it's a bid that they'll refrain from said action in the future.

"Sorrey" at the end of the day, simply holds more weight.

"But Mac," you might ask "how do I know that they'll understand the depth of their request for forgiveness?"

Easy.

In order for me to accept a "sorrey," it needs to be accompanied by a bottle of maple syrup.

Almost all of my kids are driven by material items: their iPhones, laptops, purses, sneakers, etc., so it's imperative that they have a real, tactile example that can serve to highlight their negatives as well as their positives.

The sheer act of putting things in a physical context gives their contrition merit. Plus, given that we live in a "virtual world," they're on board with actually having a real, quantifiable example of not only what they did wrong, but the fact that their "wrong" was put "right."

As it stands, I currently have two bottles on my "Sorrey" shelf. But given that it has only been

enforced for a week, I fear I'll soon need more
shelves.

Chapter 16:

"Zoom and Gloom (The Obligatory COVID Chapter)"

If the 2020-2021 school year taught us anything, collectively, the concept of "distance learning" is a fucking dumpster fire. For the majority of my students, the idea of having to use a shared connection for 6 hours a day alongside siblings and parents working from home was a logistical nightmare. Add to that, the sheer amount of mental and physical exhaustion of having to stare at a screen *and* try to read the expressions of every person in your "room."

And that's assuming that they *actually* have their screens on. Early on, I encountered students who didn't have a reliable connection, and their screens were continually lagging when we interacted. It was especially rough on students with processing and attention challenges, since they were literally missing two or more words per sentence due to lag. As soon as we offered the option for kids with bad connections to turn off their cameras, suddenly *everyone* had internet stability issues. Microphones quickly followed suit. The result was a 30+ person class with four or fewer students keeping their cameras and microphones on.

In one class, my student Greg accidentally unmuted himself, and for the next couple minutes, I could hear hollow clicks and frustrated gasps. When class was over, I asked him to stay behind.

"Tell me, Greg: what PS4 game were you playing?" Absolute silence. He tried to think quickly, and all that came out was "well, uh...I...uh...can you repeat the question?"

"Well, you had the controller close to your microphone, and it clicked a lot more solidly than the stock Xbox controllers do, so my thoughts are it was either a third party Xbox controller or a PS4. I'm leaning towards PS4 because..."

"It was *Spider-Man*" he said, awed, in a near whisper.

"Ha! I *knew* it was a PS4 controller! So the bigger question: how often are you doing this?"

"Pretty much every day," he replied glumly.

"Which would explain why you haven't gotten class participation points or turned in homework in weeks, despite daily reminders?"

"Yes."

"Ok, well I'm beyond stoked that you were honest with me. But now you know that *I* know. So if you're not on cam or muted or not answering..."

"...You know I'm playing *Spider-Man*."

"You got it, bud! With this great power..."

I'd love to tell you that I saw an incredible uptick in productivity from him, and I did! But it lasted for less than two weeks, and it was back to PS4 and mic/cam off. I can't really blame him. I was a teenager with poor impulse control and a short attention span, and this was *before* the Internet. If I was told to stay in my room for classes *and* had unfettered access to the internet, and some of the world's most high-res games, I'd have a 0.4 GPA too!

I can honestly say that 90% of my parents were great through this; they realized how much we were trying to support the kids, and doing whatever we could to meet them at their level (like dropping off printed copies of digital assignments to them because their internet went down for a week). And I could hear the exasperation in their voices, as they dealt with *their* clients and bosses via Zoom.

The biggest problem for a lot of kids was that it took a lot of work to connect with their peers over Zoom, especially when many kids chose just to have their name on a black screen instead of an avatar. Hell, there were some kids I had been working with all year who I literally saw for the first time in May, since I never saw their faces or heard their voices online.

Back in my bar security days, a guy came in and introduced himself to me and said "Nice to meet you. I don't care enough about you to remember your name." And I was slightly taken aback[22]. He laughed, then explained. He was a sociologist, and another social scientist discovered that if you made someone visually disappointed, you would equate that look with their name and subconsciously never forget. "We're basically chimps," he said "and we are constantly pattern-seeking when reading people's faces. When you disappoint someone, there's a primal part of you that doesn't want to be kicked out of the group, and wants to do everything in your power to *stay in their good graces.* So yeah, it's just subconscious negative reinforcement to force your brain to remember someone." I don't know if all that's true, but damned if it doesn't help *me* remember!

I can't tell you the absolute burnout of staring at a screen for seven hours a day with kids, bookended by one-on-one student meetings, and lunchtime FaceTime meetings on top of it. I heard someone say that the reason we're so exhausted after spending an entire day on Zoom is because we unconsciously spend our time half-listening to whatever the main person is saying, and the rest of the time scanning peoples' faces for cues, thanks to our pattern-seeking chimp brains. Are their brows furrowed? Maybe they're confused. Are they trying to talk, but accidentally on mute? Did they just roll their eyes...or are they just looking at something else in the room? Now multiply that by puberty and teenage uncertainty--it's no shock that so many kids signed in and just walked away from their computers. Or played *Spider-Man*.

There was an *incredibly* niche group, however, who flourished in distance learning. I had students that struggled to physically wake up, shower, dress themselves, eat breakfast and go to school every day during "normal" school; kids with less than half attendance for the school year, and kids who were up at 3 a.m. just to make it to school on time. I had kids that were grappling with depression, anxiety and time management, and others who were so self-critical that they couldn't ever be satisfied with their own work, so they just never turned anything in. All of these amazing, neurodivergent kiddos absolutely *crushed* it during distance learning--some earning straight A's for the first time in their lives.

It was genuinely amazing to watch growth in students who would previously wilt at the idea of having to answer a question aloud in class, suddenly able to destroy deadlines when they could complete their work on their own schedule. Suddenly they're making A's and B's and they started chasing the high of getting positive responses to their work. From there, it was just a matter of helping them build out daily work timelines, and incorporate daily "outside" time away from screens. We would use phone apps and calendar reminders to build schedules with alarms. That little executive function boost was the missing piece, and now that we had time to explore those options, the kids were *soaring*.

None of that would have been possible during a traditional school year. I get it: by and large distance learning via Zoom was a horrible experience for most people, but *without* it those students might have failed their senior year.

All of that being said, I am still waiting to hear of a single district that universally did well over Zoom. We all had a collective year+ to build out a consistent, achievable curriculum for our students throughout America, and we completely biffed it. Instead of innovating, I saw lots of teachers treading water and literally running out the clock between vacations. It was honestly challenging when the playbook would change week to week, and teachers were forced to adjust on the fly constantly; it legit felt like we were building the plane as we were flying it.

District heads in televised community meetings said things like "no student will fail this year" at the beginning of the pandemic, and kids and their parents ran with it. Even in 2021, there were teachers that would generously curve grades in order to get out of yet another shitty parent meeting.

I get it--I was there, but literally seeing teachers throw up their hands and just say *"fuck it, all F's are C's!"* was far from the best possible way to promote growth and learning.

The truth is, you had to lean into the discomfort and frustration, and actively work to build something new to bring students back into the fold. Some of the best examples of this were incorporating tactile elements into normal lessons; I knew teachers that would either deliver materials to students (or leave them in a pick-up bin in the main office), with simple things like spring scales, papercraft "constructables" or seed packets for kids to build a mini-greenhouse. We had some teachers showing kids how to build DIY kettlebell sets out of canned vegetables and reusable shopping bags, and others who combined chemistry with cooking, in an attempt to discover the perfect spaghetti sauce recipe.

Great teachers were able to figure out a way to gather the kids at the beginning of the workday, explain the expectations for the lesson, then send kids out to work, open breakout rooms for group work sessions and hang back in the main room in case kids wanted to drop in and ask questions. The trick was to get kids *away from the computer* while still encouraging them to come back at the end of the day (or at lunch, during breaks, etc.) to demonstrate learning and ask questions. Lots of teachers I know embraced Google Voice, which allowed parents and students phone/text access to us, while maintaining a safe boundary by using Google's randomly generated phone number system. Just by knowing that they could text us to check in during the day, students were suddenly more invested in group conversations, and were actually building Discord rooms to hang out with their peers during open work time.

Now that we're apparently facing a new variant every year, I'm curious how many teachers actually learned from their time in the Zoom gulag--and how many will actively innovate if classes go back online again.

For now, we're back in classes and things are...*different*. A quick scan of social media finds teachers bemoaning the state of schools, and leaving (or threatening to leave) in droves. I get it...really I do. Regardless of your stance on distance learning or in-class learning, it's painfully obvious that the kids went through a massive change over the 18ish months of "virtual learning" and classrooms are most definitely different.

The kids have become, for lack of a better word, *feral.*

In the words of one proud 17-year-old I work with: "I went from waking up at 9 a.m., logging in (with my screen and mic off), snoozing more, having a snack, searching the 'Hub (*hurk*), playing a couple matches of Warzone, then finishing my easy-ass homework before going back to CoD. Now that I have to go back again, I don't think I like school anymore."

During distance/hybrid learning, I noticed a huge bloom of new compensatory strategies from both neurotypical *and* neuroatypical students; they learned that when the bar is lowered, all they need to do is complete the base level of work, and phone in a couple "participation" comments, and blammo! Instant B...maybe even B+!

More than that, I've seen a massive uptick in Tech-Decks (the tiny, finger-operated skateboards), a scary overreliance on their phones, and a generally terrible view of authority figures (namely parents and teachers). When nobody has a face to read, and all of Zoom are just black squares with names, it saps your ability to be human. And with teenagers (and even younger kids) that are just barely learning the complex dance of meaningful social skills; this sets them all back several years.

There isn't a day that goes by where I'm not shocked by the offhanded comments that students just blurt into the air, and are only aware that they're "bad" when everyone around them stares and laughs uncomfortably.

I'm aware that all have it in us to be toxic people and blurt out inappropriate things. Sometimes, our lizard brain kicks in and fires off something, and we instantly go "oh NOOOOOO" and perseverate on it for the rest of the day (and years later, at night when we have insomnia). The problem with so many of these kids, is that they're not used to reading peoples' responses, so there's no mental governor to tell them "oh shit, that was *definitely* the wrong thing to say!"

Similarly, kids are taking their cues on what to be offended by from TikTok and other social media sites. For example, a group of kids recently bullied another quiet, soft-spoken student because of his shirt (which he bought from a major online skate-shop). The shirt featured a classic Japanese design, and had a blue sunburst in the background--reminiscent of typical 80s Japanese pop-art. The kids called him a racist and a fascist and demanded that he remove his shirt, because he was promoting fascism. When we pressed the group later, none of them could give clear historical information on *why* they were upset, nor did they offer to educate him on how his shirt could be construed as inappropriate. Upon further digging, the kids referred to a case of a YouTube/Tiktok star who came under fire for having a classic Japanese rising sun symbol as the backdrop of a tattoo. Even with that information, the students still refused to apologize to the kid...or recant their statements. "They need to know that the Japanese imperials killed like *almost like a thousand* 'other' people during their reign."

Excuse me, *what?*

As I mentioned before, kids aren't looking up things anymore, *especially* if they can just click a 20 second video that tells them how to feel...or what to be outraged at.

Good teachers realized pretty quickly that we all needed to hit the reset button, and now we're focusing on rebuilding our school community and academic relationship by taking time to re-learn about each other--staff *and* students. The emphasis during these meetings is on interpersonal communication, and we take attendance by having students put their phones in numbered pockets that we hang on the wall in front of the class. We have them go on walks and conduct empathy interviews with each other, all in an attempt to rebuild their communication skills--and relearn how to interact with each other. We gently push them to share their ideas in class, regardless if they're the right or wrong answer, so that we can use them as a jumping-off point to explain *why* their reasoning might be wrong. After all, if one student is brave enough to volunteer a potentially wrong answer, it'll not only help them, but all the other kids in class who might have had the same reasoning.

As I mentioned before, one of the best new moves for me is to co-construct classroom norms from the get-go; mainly because so many kids came back with an abject apathy for teachers (and school in general). By having the kids build their own set of expectations, we were able to set a groundwork of ownership. This way, when the kids act out (and shit starts to go sideways), we can just point at the list of rules at the front of the class. It's surprising how much kids will self-police when they can see themselves as active participants in the learning process.

Chapter 17:

"Summertiiiime, And The Living's...
Incredibly Difficult, Actually"

"How hard can being a teacher be? You get two months off while the rest of us actually have to work!"

I can't tell you how many times I have heard that over the years, but it has to be in the triple digits. I feel like the general public are horribly misinformed: yes, there's no school for approximately 45 days in the summer, but for substitutes, that's time you aren't getting paid. Ditto for holiday break, spring break, thanksgiving break and the other odd days off that teachers and admin get throughout the calendar year. Many young subs compete with teenagers for "vacation jobs," usually in food service or the bar industry.

I know I mentioned it before, but it bears repeating: I worked on and off in bars for three years while subbing just to make ends meet. Four days a week I would teach from 7 a.m. to 3:30 p.m., then work at the bar from 6:00 p.m. to 3:00 a.m., and be back in the classroom at 7 a.m. It's definitely a routine that a mid-20s to early-30s body could do, but I *definitely* couldn't pull that off these days.

I'd always try to beef up my availability during holiday and summer breaks, but companies weren't exactly falling over themselves to hire someone who worked two and a half months out of the year. Because of this, I tried to sock aside whatever money I could during these "lean" months. And summertime means everyone and their mother want to go outside, do group vacations, and have backyard BBQs. During these years, discount grocery and warehouse outlet stores became my go-to for food. Hell, even nowadays when I find myself driving by a Big Lots on my way to a proper grocery store, I feel like I'm driving past a last-call hook-up barfly, as she takes a long drag off of a Marlboro Light 100, hocks a loogie and growls *"hiya handsome! I know you'll be back for my deals. They alllllllways come back!"*

The term "vacation" is a bit of a misnomer, as many districts contract their teachers through the *actual* work months, and the summer often tends to be unpaid (in a manner of speaking). Add to that, many teachers use this time to reset their classrooms, build curriculum and plan out the first half of the next school year. And there's the whole "resetting your brain" to *not* wake up at 5 a.m. to start getting ready to teach. Usually, you break that habit when you're *just* about to return to classes, which is always super neat.

There's also the rapid slide from "another glass of wine with dinner *'because it's summer and I don't teach in the morning'*" to "okay, so *how* terrible is day drinking four days in a row, *really*? Isn't it like a 'four on, one off' rule?"

Also, summer is when many substitutes (particularly those under 40) try to pick up extra teaching assignments by running summer school classes. I'd venture a guess to say that most summer school teachers decide to teach it sometime in May. And if we're being honest, there's a reason why the 80s Mark Harmon movie was so popular--*because it's pretty damn spot-on.*

I'm sure *every* teacher kicks off summer school with the best of intentions. But remember: this isn't a typical classroom. Summer school tends to be a who's who of challenging kids from the regular school year–only this time, it's an entire class full. So after the first week, the physical and mental burnout kicks in, and suddenly we're watching History Channel documentaries and answering short essay questions. Week two is *Ancient Aliens* and a pizza party. Week three is usually when the *I don't care what they're doing, as long as they're not doing anything illegal* line of demarcation gets drawn.

And really, who could blame you? There's no feasible way to jam in all of the content that they failed the first time around, and short of having them do an open-book revision of their failed tests (which I've *totally* done), so you're hitting a wall by the start of week two. There's a pretty significant drop off on the "fucks given" scale by the end of *that* week, and then it's a headlong plunge into "what are some acceptable Netflix movies I can show kids for the rest of this godforsaken session?"

One summer, completely thinking outside the box, I offered to teach a "Film as Literature: Journey into the Unknown" class for 9-12th grade English credit recovery. It was *amazing*. I sent home a list of titles that I was thinking about showing:

Reservoir Dogs

Training Day

The Thing

Henry V

Blazing Saddles

Aliens

The Godfather

Charlie and the Chocolate Factory

Tropic Thunder

Evil Dead

Cabin in the Woods

The parent response was astounding; not only did I include my phone number and email address, I also left space for them to write any notes or suggestions. One wrote "Can I take your class?" another said "Sounds *RAD!!!*" and literally every parent signed. I did field one concerned call from a mother, who asked "I know those movies are mostly all R-rated, but is there sex in any of them?" I said "Well, there's some in Godfather and brief nudity in others." She thought about it for a minute, then replied "well ok. As long as there's no porno stuff, I'm ok with it." And *that* may have been the quote of the summer.

It went swimmingly: I spent the entire first day explaining the hero's journey concept and drew a giant circle out on the dry erase board to refer to all week. I would start each morning with a writing prompt ("*what character archetypes are present in Cabin in the Woods? How do they fit into the hero's journey? What other tropes do you notice?*"), and we would watch the movie, break it down at the halfway mark and take notes on the board. They would then spend the afternoon writing and analyzing what they watched. Not only did they display learning, but they would peer-review each other's work, strengthening their editing abilities. Hell, I knew we'd probably end up watching movies anyway, *so why not build it into the lesson plan?*

If summer school is an educational wash, why not teach something you love? I taught the "hero's journey" summer class three more times, and I was shocked each time I got paid for it. Then again, there were quantifiable results, and the kids essentially ended up being tricked into learning and applying content. Win/win.

Speaking of boundaries and not good things: in my second year of teaching summer school, in the last week of classes, I had a parent ask to speak with me first thing in the morning when she walked her 10th-grade son to my room.

It was one of the long classrooms with an office in the back, the board at the front, and a big picture window that looked into the office itself.

The mom was dressed like she was heading to spin class after (it was mid-July and this was par for the course with lots of parents), and I brought her back to my office. I assumed that she had questions about his behavior and the updates I was sending home.

The kid was a total wiseass but SUPER smart, and was legit just bored in his classes. He was only in summer school because he ditched the majority of English classes throughout the school year. So I told him if he did all of his reading and writing work at the beginning of the day, he could chill for the last two hours, and that's what he did...every single day.

I walked into the small office, to show her his work portfolio and she closed the door behind her. "It's really important that he pass this English class so we can go on vacation before school starts again," she said, and began to pull the zipper on her jacket down. She wasn't wearing a top under it.

My face went beet red as I looked out the window of the office at the kids filtering in. I took a comically loud gulp of air as she smirked at me.

"*HAVEYOUEVENCHECKEDHISGRADESHE'SDOINGFINEANDHAS ALLHISWORKINANDIHAVETOSTARTCLASSOK?!?*"

In my haste to blurt out his academic standing, I ended up shouting at her...as all the kids whirled around to see what the hell was happening in my office.

She yanked the jacket zipper up and stormed out in a huff.

As I followed her down the class aisle, her kid looked at me and said "your face is all red. Did she yell at you or something?"

"Or something."

I was dazed for the rest of the class. Like, how often has she done that in the past? And to what degree? Poor kid.

Chapter 18:

"A Generic, Feel Good Ending"

The number one thing I want you to take away from this book, is that no matter how much I've taught over the years, it's the kids that were truly teaching me all along.[23]

If you ever hear me say that in real life, I want you to punch me in the fucking face as hard as you can. I'm not kidding. I won't even press charges![24]

Being a teacher and saying that aloud (and *meaning* it) is like crucifying yourself on a bunch of those shitty, rustic "Live, Laugh, Love" planks from HomeGoods. It's the educational equivalent of saying "Candyman" three times into the mirror of a darkened bathroom. Only this time, a pre-teen appears behind you with yet *another* "World's BEST Teacher" mug...and then promptly sneezes into your mouth.

But I digress.

Here's the actual takeaway: no matter what you're doing in this life, the best thing you can do for yourself is be self-reflective. I know you've seen a lot of cringe in these stories, but I also hope you see a lot of growth. I make no bones about it: I was a pretty shit teacher at the beginning, and I honestly consider myself a damned good one now...but self-improvement is the name of the game. Document your days, and review your progress. Set personal goals, and try to do one small thing better each week.

One of the best things you can do is get out of your comfort zone and observe another badass teacher. Kid falling asleep in your class? See how they act in other classrooms. Maybe there's a new tweak or strategy you can try out! I can't tell you how many new things I've picked up from sitting in on another class of a different discipline. Do I think I'm the best? Of *course* I do! But there's always room to get better. At the very least, you can try to hone your craft from a different angle!

Surround yourself with people who will call you out on your bullshit. Sycophants are great, but you can't get better living in a complacent echo chamber. Do lesson studies and project tuning. Click up with teachers who have similar mindsets, and challenge each other on lesson planning. Try to pick a group of teacher friends who will help lift you up--and try to do the same for them. *And never take yourself too seriously.*

There are too many good "new" teachers that never learn to cut themselves a break, and end up drowning in the ocean of self-imposed and systemic expectations. Keep an eye out for new teaching talent, and for God's sake *nurture and support it!* I said it before and I'll say it again: this industry is full of people that are happy to coast through content and bury kids in packet work. A *great* teacher will keep trying new and engaging things. And when you see that spark in a potential new teacher, do everything you can to support them.

At the end of the day, if you're doing everything you can to support the kids, you will *"sleep the sleep of the just."* But speaking of sleep: set boundaries, go to sleep at a normal time, eat your vitamins (*"AND SAY YOUR PRAYERS, BROTHER!"*), and remember to take time to breathe. *And never ever ever EVER read parent emails after 5 p.m.*[25] Save that shit for 7 a.m. tomorrow!

This part is crucial: **you need to aggressively pursue joy each day**. That might be a walk around the building during your planning period, or sneaking out to your car to jam out to your theme song for a couple minutes. Nurturing kids is physically and emotionally exhausting, and you need to remember to add kindling to your own fire--you can't support others if you're not taking care of yourself.

And, like all things in life: if it stops being rewarding and enjoyable *fucking quit and do something else!* I mean, have something else lined up, of course...but if you're not feeling like it's the best possible fit for you, try going somewhere else! Shit, I was almost 40 before becoming a "for realsies" teacher, but before that, I believed that I would die an editor with every fiber of my being.

When you start hating your job and your coworkers, *you will inadvertently start hating your students*, and that poisons the well for everyone involved.

If you're *not* a teacher, help out someone that is! Donate shelf-stable breakfast food to classrooms, or send your kid into class with a couple boxes of granola bars to add to the pot. Encourage class pantries, where kids can take what they need (tissues, deodorant, mouthwash, toothbrushes, etc.) without feeling like they're getting a handout. Ditto for supplies like markers, pens, tape, glue and pencils. Dear lord, teaching is the *only* job on earth where you steal supplies from home to bring to work with you.

And for fuck's sake, can we quit with the $5 Starbucks cards every couple months? We teachers are smart, but tracking and organizing our piles of gift cards is tedious...and I can't tell you how many times I've gone to pay with the "$20" card in my wallet, only to find that it has 32 cents left on it[26]. Seriously, a couple nice gift cards for food/booze per year would be great. Hell, one year I had a legendary parent give me a *super* fancy bottle of tequila and a bunch of infused dipping oils during the holidays, and I haven't stopped thinking about it since. The only thing she wrote on the card was *"you probably need this by now <3 ."* Yes, I know: *not everyone drinks.* So maybe just a grocery store gift card. Or a gift certificats for a massage. Or better yet, have your kid write/draw something for our desk; I can't tell you how much a heartfelt letter from a kiddo means to me.

Even without that, if you're a parent, just try to be kind and patient with us. Give us 48 hours to reply to your emails, and don't expect replies after business hours, and don't call after hours...I mean, unless your kid is on fire. And even if that's the case, you should probably call 9-1-1 or the fire department before calling me, because I'm useless. I'll probably just end up yelling "STOP DROP AND ROLLL!" at you repeatedly.

Most of us teachers think the world of your kid(s), and we will fight just as hard for them as we would for our own.[27] We do this because we love it, and we want you to remember that no matter how wonky it appears, we're on the same team.

I can honestly say that my incredible parents beat out my not-so-great parents 50 to 1, and even though we don't always say it, we see you:

- Parents working two full-time jobs to give your kids a better life.
- Parents trying to get a houseful of kids dressed, fed and out the door on time every day.
- Parents who aren't fluent English speakers but are trying their hardest to keep in touch.
- Parents who can't reach their kids, but just want to know

how they're *really* doing.
- And every other parent in between. We see you.

Unless, of course, we see you out at a bar, or in the mosh pit at a show, or when we're hungover in a Target checkout line at 8 a.m. on a Sunday in scummy jeans and a stained shirt, desperately clutching a bottle of Bloody Mary mix and a pack of bacon. Then we *definitely* don't see you, and would love it if you returned the favor.

I wanted to close the book with an inspirational quote, but instead, I'll leave you with my daily goodbye to my kiddos:

"Get outta here! Have a great day! Go outside! Do stuff! Take risks! Be awesome! And don't die!"

Acknowledgements

Holy shit! You made it to the end! Look at you!

I know there are some people who I missed in the dedication (and I probably missed a whole lot more here. So I'll leave a blank line at the end to add yourself.

Thank you to all of these amazing teachers I have had the honor of working alongside. You have not only inspired me to be a better teacher, but you've inspired so many of your students to greatness!

> **Mark W.** - *the lessons I have learned from you are innumerable. Thank you for your continual belief, even when I didn't give you much to work with.*

> **Amanda C.** - *the best damn mentor a guy could ever hope for. Thank you for believing and guiding me...especially when you didn't have to.*

> **Ady K.** - *thank you for being my partner and my rock year one. You are the exemplar of what a dean and advisor can be.*

> **Sarah B.** - *thank you for always believing in me, giving me my first shot, and always being a sounding board.*

> **John S.** - *one of the most kind, level-headed teachers in the*

game. Your belief in the inherent good in kids is staggering. Honored to have worked with you.

Peter J. - *every school needs an English curmudgeon, and you excelled at it, my friend.*

Joyce C. - *down since day one. I'm honored to have continually shared space, kids, and challenges with you.*

Allison D. - *the* ultimate *apprentice. You are so naturally gifted and will do amazing things. Please keep on keeping on!*

Father Dan - *the best teacher I could have asked for. Thank you for everything.*

Dennis Lambert - *in a lot of ways, you are my model for what a great English teacher should be. Rest in power.*

Mary-Ellen Pelletier - *you were always strict but fair. I hope you're watching and laughing. Thanks for always hearing me out and believing in me...even when you knew I was full of shit.*

---

[1] It should go without saying, but all names, locations, dates and identifying traits have been changed to protect the innocent.

[2] This entire exchange needs a massive (sic) disclaimer.

[3] A nearby alternative school with a reputation as the "bad kid" school. Most kids get sent there for possession of drugs, fighting and other "recidivist" behavior.

[4] Parole officers

[5] I later discovered that Dickface was what the kids called "a 'try hard'--someone that was uncomfortable in their own skin, so they put on airs to come across as more tough or cool than they were.

[6] Or, as they would call it, a "try hard" or a "pick me motherfucker"

[7] Juvie security guards

[8] When you appear to swallow your medication, but tuck it into your cheek

and spit it out when nobody's looking.

[9] It was "peanut butter and cat poop sandwiches" in case you want to kidnap me..

[10] I'm not at all speaking to those absolutely legendary parents that are raising their kid(s) single handedly while working two full time jobs.

[11] Mind you, this does not include students with exceptional needs, who sometimes utilize negative behavior as communication--I'm speaking more to the entitled neurotypical students who are making life hard for the *entire* class.

[12] A "Super Senior" is a senior that is either retaking 12th grade or is missing enough credits to necessitate an extra year of high school.

[13] Let's not kid ourselves: great teachers get stuck in ruts too, and sometimes struggle to innovate. I'm not blaming teachers that are actively struggling and failing...I'm blaming ones that stopped trying.

[14] An adult film actress of the 70s-80s.I would advise against Googling her at work.

[15] The sherpa-lined nylon parachute-like rig that kept him safe on the bus ride to and from school.

[16] In hindsight, probably not the best choice of words, but whatever.

[17] 59. It was 59 meetings. Just. This. Year. *Not* counting open houses, recitals or other "all school" events.

[18] Yeah I had to look it up too. It's a rotten-smelling tinned fish from Norway that's preserved with lye and pretty much just turns into jelly. I'm retching just typing this.

[19] I later found out that this was the teacher that would come into class hungover almost daily, and routinely wore her sunglasses indoors for the first half of the day.

[20] And teaching Midsummer without getting into Shakespeare's sneer (yet again) at the concept of marriage and the superficiality of love, don't even bother cracking the cover.

[21] The Least-Restrictive (learning) Environment

[22] But not *too* terribly taken aback--it *was* a bar, after all!

[23] Also worth noting: I'm *definitely* a hot, 30-something blonde woman with a sassy demeanor, a shiny black leather coat and bright red stiletto heels. I'm making a DIFFERENCE!

[24] I mean, unless you're *rich!*

[25] And definitely *not before bed!*

[26] I once had a kid that gave out $50 gift cards to all his teachers for Christmas, but only put a dollar on each. They didn't notice until at *least* February, simply due to all the other cards. Touche, little velociraptor.

[27] Unless they're awful. Then you owe us *twice* the gift cards and booze. And you *know* if they're awful...you **always** know.

About The Author

M. C. Shaw

MacArthur C. Shaw is an author, teacher and has been called "an utter godsend" by a couple of parents, and "pretty okay" by almost all others.

He has been teaching various "high challenge" classrooms for the last nine years, five of which were spent as Education Specialist. Like Larry Rosenstock, he is a firm believer that a child *will* do well if they *can* do well, and that with enough structure, rigor and support, we can expect the best of ALL kids.

He was arrested only once on suspicion of possessing criminal amounts of "W-Rizz," but was later released due to lack of evidence...probably on account of his Hawaiian shirt obsession.

He spends his downtime gaming, watching murder documentaries with his ever-patient wife, and playing fetch with his two psychotic rescue cats. He will also undoubtedly charm your grandmother if left unattended.

He desperately wishes he could make al pastor and birria tacos at home, but has been unsuccessful thus far.

Mmmmmmm. Tacos al pastor.

Made in the USA
Monee, IL
24 April 2023

32360130R00125